THE MORALS GAME

THE MORALS GAME

by
Edward Stevens

PAULIST PRESS
New York / Paramus / Toronto

Library of Congress
Catalog Card Number: 74-18855

ISBN: 0-8091-1852-1

Cover Design: Dan Pezza

Published by Paulist Press
Editorial Office: 1865 Broadway, N.Y., N.Y. 10023
Business Office: 400 Sette Drive, Paramus, N.J. 07652

Printed and bound in the
United States of America

CONTENTS

To my students

PREFACE

Go to the gaming tables of Las Vegas or to the soccer stadia of Brazil, and you will make no mistake about it that games can be played in dead earnest. This is a book about the "morals game." Each one of us is a player, and the "morals game" is played for keeps. The stakes are nothing less than the whole worth and meaning of my human life on earth. Because the stakes are high, a well-played game is profoundly satisfying. But it's not all fun. Decisions about the right moves are often agonizing and painful.

What is *your* book of rules? How do you make these decisions? Glance at the Table of Contents and Chapters One to Four. These are some of the ways that people play today. Where do you fit in? Here you will find the timeless moral philosophies: morality based on love, morality based on intelligence, morality based on religion. And the game is played with different mental attitudes too. Morality, for some, is a psychological growing process. For others, it's a strait-jacket in a prison or even a script played out on the human comic stage.

The first half of this book treats the morals game more like a spectator sport. However, since in this game every spectator is also a player, you'll be comparing your own style to the way the others play. You'll be asked to reflect on just what your philosophy of human life is. And the answers you come up with will throw light on how you play the morals game.

Glance now at the contents of Chapters Seven to Eleven. Things now begin to get more personal. We're no longer looking at various

1

editions of the rulebook. You're invited out of the grandstand and onto the playing field where the hard, practical, daily moral decisions are made. Here are the issues that make the daily headlines, because it is by these decisions that people stand or fall and games are won or lost. Abortion and euthanasia, quality of life versus quantity of life, respect for life versus experimentation on it and technological control —there are no easy rulebook answers. The alternatives will be presented "pro" and "con" and in-between. Test cases will be offered and you'll be invited to take a stand. There will be questionnaires on war, on justice, on sex. Maybe your answers will reveal where your values really lie. Decision and action are the test of how you really play. In this way, you can clarify for yourself the what, the why and the wherefore of *your* moral positions, for example, on amnesty for war objectors, on reverse discrimination in favor of minority groups, on the changing forms of marriage and sexuality, on the tensions between authority and freedom, and on the ecological penalties exacted by our consumer-oriented life-styles.

Why is another book needed on these questions? Haven't they been done to death? After all, the philosophies of Part One were said to be "timeless." Timeless, yes, but with a difference. Each generation ("generation" now meaning three to five years!) perceives intelligence and love, the human prison and the human comedy with its own peculiar sensibilities and concerns. What happens in psychology, sociology, anthropology, and economics cannot but shape and mold a philosophy. These sciences state the laws of practical human action, and action is the name of the game in morals. Moral philosophy cannot operate in splendid isolation. This book tries to sum up and illustrate in a short space this contemporary interdisciplinary approach to ethics.

Conversely, the more "timely" moral issues that are raised in Part Two have a timeless aspect to them. The perennial human moral tensions take on a different form in each "generation." For example, yesterday's issue of conscientious objection today translates into that of amnesty for objectors—the underlying tension between individual conscience and civil law remains the same. Yesterday's "equal opportunity for women" becomes today's "discrimination in their favor"— the underlying tension between human equality and human differences remains the same. This book attempts to focus on the precise shape of these issues as we face them today.

Finally, the purpose of the book is practical. Whether you are a reader alone, or in a discussion group, or in a classroom, it challenges you to reflect on the meaning of your own life. As a spectator, you will see how others play out their lives and will compare their style to your own. And as a participant, you will be invited to take a moral stand on the hard issues of today. What are your real values? Why do you hold them? Do you like them? In a word, how do *you* play the morals game?

Note that this book is not intended to push any particular game. I have tried to enter into the spirit of various moral games as sympathetically and even enthusiastically as possible. Enthusiasm of presentation is not to be taken as endorsement. Various games call for various philosophical hats and uniforms. We'll be changing uniforms often. In the relatively rare case that I give a personal moral opinion, I'll try to make that clear. The point is not to push my game, but to help you clarify yours as you consider representative alternative positions.

Books, periodicals, and the media's torrential "words without end" have been the input into this author's mind—a rather faulty computer. I owe it to constant challenge and dialogue with my students that the computer is not more erratic than it is. These are my unacknowledged sources. The footnotes are minimal, restricted to references explicitly made in the text. These footnotes, meager though they be, can serve as leads into topics you would like to explore further. So much for the ground rules. Let's play ball!

PART ONE

ONE: WHY SHOULD YOU?

The nations, which only yesterday were proclaiming their solidarity in the battle for the freedom of mankind, are now competing against each other for the production of atomic bombs; and who can doubt that the unthinkable of today will be the commonplace of tomorrow? What is the point, in a world situation such as this, of the ridiculous "ethical" question and the still more ridiculous answer, "It all depends on the individual"?

Erich Neumann[1]

This is a book about the game of "should." To call it a game is not to take it lightly. Like professional football, the game of "should" is often played in dead earnest, even to the point of bloodshed and war. This game is played by many different sets of rules, as we will see. Morality can put you in a psychological prison. This is when the rules of your game are written by others. You might not even realize that you are living out your life in a moral prison. Or life can be a morality play in which you choose your own roles and write your own stage directions. Two later chapters will be devoted to these views of "morality as prison" and "morality as theatre." To those who write their own moral rule books, philosophers give differing advice. Follow your heart, say some; follow your mind, others advise. We will examine these recommendations later; first we have to clear the ground. In this chapter I'll lay my cards on the table. I'll present what I consider to be the basic rules for playing any game of morals.

7

Moral rulebooks are filled with words like "good," "bad," "should," "ideal," and last but not least the "thou shalts" and the "thou shalt nots" that are alleged to issue from that ultimate arbiter of the moral ball game, the divine umpire in the sky. So let us look now at what is to be said, first about moral obligation in general, then about values and ideas.

THE MORAL EXPERIENCE

The World of "Should"

"Should" is the big club used in the moral ball game. But it's confusing. "Should" can be used in ways that have little or nothing to do with morals. And "morals": There's another loaded word. We all know what a morals charge is. And we've all heard preachers lashing out against immorality, by which they seem to mean fornication, pornography, loose women, and sex in general. So morality has acquired the bad reputation of being anti-sex. This reputation is libelous on two counts. First, sex plays a small and relatively minor part in the world of morality. And secondly, morality has much more to do with being *pro* something than with being *anti* anything. But we'll come to that later. Let's get back to "should."

There are some things I should do, *depending*. There are other things I should do, *period*. The first kind of "should" is called hypothetical. There's a big *if* about it. The second kind of "should" is called categorical. There are no ifs, ands, or buts about it. The first kind of "should" has nothing to do with morality. The second kind of "should" describes our experience of moral obligation.

Let's look at the first type of "should," the type of obligation that depends on a big *if*. Here are some examples. I have to wear shoes if I want to eat at the hotel coffee shop. They won't let me in otherwise. So I ask: should I wear shoes? Your answer, yes—*if* you want to eat there. Another example: Don't go to bed with Times Square prostitutes if you want to avoid V.D. Well, suppose I put my trust in antibiotics and don't care about catching the clap? If this is the case, then there is no obligation to avoid the prostitutes; the obligation was hypothetical. In other words, this particular "should" was conditioned by whether or not I wanted to risk catching a venereal disease. A final example: Should I put an illegal wiretap on my competitor's phone? Answer: Yes, if I want to outbid him on the next contract.

The question of "should" or obligation was raised regarding three actions: wearing shoes, whoring, and wiretapping. The answer in each case was: "It depends." In each case, the obligation involved was hypothetical. If you wanted to accomplish a certain end (eat in a coffee shop, avoid V.D., outbid a competitor), then this is what you had to do (wear shoes, avoid prostitutes, wiretap). These questions were not treated as *moral* issues. Moral obligation is not a matter of *if*. In other words, moral obligation is experienced not as hypothetical, but as categorical.

Categorical means unconditioned, without any ifs, ands, or buts. To the moral question—"Should I whore around?"—the moral answer is experienced as "no," period (or "yes," period). Whether or not I want to risk disease is peripheral and not directly relevant to the moral issue. Similarly, wiretapping as a moral issue is experienced as morally wrong, period (or morally right, period). Whether or not I want to outbid my competitor is not directly relevant to the moral issue involved.

Hypothetical obligations have to do with expediency. Moral obligation cuts much deeper than expediency. Moral obligation is categorical. In other words, it is not conditioned by what is expedient. Moral obligation has to do with the kind of human being you want to be. Well, how do you decide whether whoring or wiretapping or even wearing shoes is morally good or morally evil? This will be the subject of the rest of the book. But we want to make it clear right off that more than expediency is involved. In moral matters, what is at stake is the very meaning of your life as a human being. That is why moral obligation is not hypothetical and conditioned, but categorical and absolute.

Good and Bad

This becomes clearer when we consider the meaning of the words "good" and "bad." Again, these words are confusing. They are used in many ways that have nothing to do with morality. Joe Passerman, star quarterback, can have a lousy game. The fans boo, and the sportswriters call him a *bad* player. But when he gets home, his wife tells him: "I don't care what they say, honey, you're a *good* man." Teenage tennis prodigy Tenney Raquet wins her first tournament. Her grandmother reminds her: "You may be a *good* tennis player, but remember, the important thing is to be a *good* woman." Gus Glibtongue might be a *good* salesman, the best his company has on the East Coast, but the methods he uses may well give him the reputation of being a *bad* human being.

So quarterbacks, tennis players, and salesmen can be good or bad at what they do. But being good *at* something has nothing to do with morality. This may seem obvious, but is it? How often do we hold up as moral models the wealthy businessman, the powerful politician, or the star athlete? The banker is admired as a pillar of the community. The political leader's exhortations to virtue make the headlines, and the star athlete is interviewed about his opinion concerning the morality of drugs and war. Granted, a banker may be *good at* making money, a president *good at* political infighting, and an athlete *good at* passing a football. But being good at a particular kind of activity does not necessarily make for a morally good human being. But you'd never realize this by looking at the results of the annual poll concerning the ten persons most admired by Americans. We tend to confuse moral good with success, with achievement in a particular field, with being good at some thing.

Moral good cuts much deeper than success in a particular field of activity. Moral good involves nothing less than success as a human being. Occasionally this is brought home to us by the shock of the banker committing suicide, or the athletic star revealed as a drug-pusher, or the president as involved in corruption. Morally good actions are actions that are in harmony with my being a fully human person. Morally good actions involve more than this or that particular skill that I might have. I am morally good when I am true to myself with all my potential and in all my relationships. Conversely, morally evil actions are those which are untrue to myself, which are not in harmony with what it means to be a full human being. Well, how do I tell what it means to be a full human being? Again, this is the subject of the rest of the book. But we want to make it clear right off that moral good involves more than being good at something. In moral matters, what is at stake is the very meaning of your life as a human being.

This book challenges you to look at your philosophy of life. Religion by itself isn't enough to understand the meaning of morality, as we'll see in the next chapter. Philosophy is what is required of you. Maybe you've never spelled or pronounced the word philosophy before, but you have a philosophy of life, and it guides all your actions. Nothing is more practical than your philosophy of life. Maybe you've given no more thought to your philosophy than you have to your heartbeat. But your philosophy is the heartbeat of your moral life.

Wouldn't it be a good idea to figure out what it is and see if you like it or want to change it for the better?

Science Is Not Enough

How to figure out what your philosophy of life is will become clearer as we go on. It's not just psychology we're talking about. It's not just sociology. These are not enough. Let's see why.

Of course, psychology will have a lot to tell us about our moral behavior and how it develops. Exactly how much we will see especially in Chapter Two. It can describe the differences in the way children, adolescents and adults approach moral decisions. Psychology not only describes moral behavior, but it forms hypotheses to explain the data it describes. For example, the Freudian superego is a hypothesis formed in part to explain the origin of guilt feelings and of the moral taboos we experience. Educational psychology describes how values are taught and experiments with ways of implanting moral feelings in the child or changing them in the adult. Social psychology distinguishes morally conforming behavior from morally deviant behavior in a society and determines the effects of each and how they might be controlled. What is there left for a moral *philosophy* to do?

Scientific psychology describes moral behavior and forms hypotheses to explain and control it. But in order to operate, the scientific psychologist must *presuppose* certain things about the world and about the human beings he is studying. In other words, scientific investigation necessarily presupposes a philosophy of life, a philosophy of man. This is where philosophy comes in. Philosophy examines the truth or falsity of what science presupposes. For purposes of investigation, for example, the scientist might assume that conforming moral behavior is "healthier" than deviant moral behavior, that moral actions are in principle not free but causally determined and completely predictable, and that there is sufficient order and sense in the world of human action to make it worthwhile to look for its laws. What moral psychology *assumes*, moral philosophy *examines*. For example, this scientist in his philosophical moments might ask himself: Is it true that conforming behavior is healthier than deviant behavior? Can human actions be genuinely free? Does the world make sense or do we live in a basically absurd universe? These are philosophical questions, not susceptible to scientific examination, but demanding investigation nonetheless. So psychology will be useful to you as you examine your own moral life, but the philosophy underlying your moral life cuts deeper than psychology. These deeper basic questions form the main thrust of this book.

Sociology, also, will have a lot to tell us about our moral behavior. Chapter Three will draw heavily on the findings of sociologists. They describe how moral beliefs arise in a society, what methods are used to make these beliefs credible and maintain them, and how the structure of different societies shapes the morality of these societies. Like the psychologist, the sociologist must make certain assumptions to get his investigation off the ground. The psychologist, for the sake of his method, might assume that moral actions are causally determined and then proceed to look for these causes. The sociologist, for the sake of his method, might assume that moral actions are socially determined and then proceed to investigate what these social determinants are. This is perfectly legitimate. But you, as you reflect on the philosophy underlying your moral life, can't afford to stay at that level. A scientific assumption made for the sake of investigation is *not* a philosophical statement about the way things are. So you can't follow the psychologist and say, "All my moral decisions are causally determined, so it doesn't matter what I do." The philosopher in you must ask whether this is really the case. You can't sit back, bathed in the light of sociology, and say: "All morals are relative; it depends on the society I was raised in." The philosopher in you must ask whether this is really the case. A philosophical statement about the way things are is different from a scientific assumption. What is at stake in your moral life is your whole philosophy of what it means to be a human being.

This book invites you to reflect on your own morality. We have begun, therefore, with the moral experience and have pointed out three of its characteristics. First, moral obligation is felt to be unconditional. Morality is more than mere expediency. Secondly, moral good involves goodness as a whole human being. It is more than being good *at* something. Morality cuts deeper than mere success. Thirdly, your moral decisions are based on something deeper than what you can learn from the hypothetical-deductive method of psychology and sociology. These three characteristics are three ways of saying simply this: To examine your moral life means to examine your philosophy of life—what does it mean for you to be a human being? At stake are your most fundamental values as a human being. "Values" is to be the topic of the next section. What are values? How are values related to ideals? What's special about moral values?

THE WORLD OF VALUES

Wishes Versus Wishy-Washies

In the matter of values, people deceive themselves in two ways—first, when they think they don't have values, but they really do; and secondly, when they think they value something, but they really don't. The self-styled "objective" scientist or "objective" professor is an example of the first kind of self-deception. We have come to see that so-called value-free science or value-free education is an illusion. Take the scientist, for example, who is developing lethal viruses for bacteriological warfare. Less and less has he been able to maintain the pose: "I just work here in a biological laboratory; what the government intends to do with my work is no concern of mine." What the scientist chooses to do or chooses not to do has an inevitable impact on the quality of human life, which is to say on the world of value. More and more, education has dropped the pose of being value-free. Take the professor, for example, who claims to look at religion "objectively." How often does the cloak of objectivity hide from the professor himself that he is actually preaching against religious commitment. Religion comes to be treated not objectively, but as a *dis*value. We said before that, whether you realize it or not, you do have a philosophy of life that guides your moral decisions. We can now add that, whether you realize it or not, you do have a set of values expressed by your actions and formed by your actions. And that goes for scientists and educators as well as the man in the street. And since my values are the measure of myself as a human being, it is crucial that I make clear to myself just what my values really are. The man who knows the price of everything and the value of nothing is a moral monster.

The second type of self-deception gets in the way of this process of values clarification. It's so easy to kid myself into thinking that I value something, when I really don't value it at all. Take a person who says, for example: "Reading is very important to me; in fact, daily reading should be a part of every adult's life." It sounds as if reading is a value to him. But what would you think if you knew that he hadn't cracked a book or even a newspaper in years, and that he spent every spare, waking moment in front of the boob tube? You would say, and rightly, that television is a value to him, not reading. He *would like* reading to be a value. The technical term for a mere "would like" is a *velleity*, or call it a wishy-washy. A velleity is something I would like, but I'm not prepared to act on it. A value is something that I consistently act upon. Action is the acid test of value.

Psychologist Louis Raths[2] has described seven steps that go into the making of a real value; if any of these steps is missing, then the alleged value is no more than just a velleity. The first step is obvious. A value is something you *prize* and *cherish*. A broken down car you're trying to unload on an unsuspecting buyer is not a value to you. But cherishing in secret is not enough. The second step is that you must be willing, when appropriate, to *publicly affirm* what you value. A girl rightly suspects your sincerity when you tell her that you love her but don't want to be seen publicly with her. Third, there must be the possibility of freedom, i.e., available *alternatives*. Which do you believe really values a clean environment—steel company X which has installed anti-pollution devices under threat of severe fines, or steel company Y which has initiated its own anti-pollution program? Fourth, a true value is chosen *intelligently*, after a consideration of the consequences. For whom is wine a real value: for the teenager who has unwittingly drunk himself unconscious, or for the connoisseur who savors the bouquet and the taste of each sip? Fifth, a value is something that I choose *freely*, after intelligent consideration from available alternatives. The sixth and seventh steps in the formation of a true value involve *acting* on your beliefs, not just acting, but acting on them *repeatedly* and with a *consistent pattern*. In summary, a value is something that I really and sincerely prize and cherish; otherwise it is just a velleity. Further, I choose it with intelligence and freedom. Otherwise, appearances to the contrary, it is not a true value at all. But the final test of value is action. Do I consistently *act* on what I claim to freely cherish and intelligently choose? If you want to know what your real moral values are, look at your actions.

One way of getting in touch with your actions, and hence with your values is by making out a Values Time Sheet.[3] Time is your most precious commodity. What you spend it on is a good indicator of what you value. Take a paper and pencil, and go over your activities of the past twenty-four hours, half hour by half hour. After filling out this time diary, consider what you actually used your time on. Do this a few times and you'll have a pretty good idea of your priorities, your hierarchy of values. Children, career, meals, commuting, television, shopping, alcohol, neighbors, sleep: As the minutes of your life roll by, who receives their benefit? On what activities are they spent? In the matter of values, it's hard to argue with the test of action. I can *say*, for example, that my children are the most important thing in life to me. I assure my son that I really care about how he's doing in the Little League. But he rightly looks at me with a skeptical eye when every Saturday afternoon in the battle for my time, the game on television invariably wins out over the game at the Little League park.

Money is another excellent barometer of where values really lie. This is part of conventional wisdom. "Put your money where your mouth is," we say. Consider a congressman posing as a friend of the poor. He votes against a food stamp program in favor of increased military spending. The allocation of money speaks of his values louder than do his words. So does your household budget. Why is a second car a necessity of life for you but not for your neighbor across the street? Why are nicotine and alcohol on your budget when another family won't have them in the house? Out of two families alike in most respects, why is one content to live in an apartment while the other takes the financial burden of a house with an immense mortgage? Each monetary decision is really a decision about values. You say that you love the simple life. Do you *live* the simple life?

In this section we have made two points. First, you can't be completely disinterested, "objective," and value-free. If you think you are, you deceive yourself. Whether you know it or not, a value system underlies your beliefs and actions. The task is to clarify what your value system is. The second point we made is simply this: Action is the acid test of value. How you use your time and your money will give you an accurate idea of where your values really lie.

What about those things which I truly cherish, but which I simply cannot yet translate into action? I value world peace, the eradication of hunger, perfect communication with my wife, perfect honesty with myself. Are these values to be called phony simply because they do not pass the test of action? How do *ideals* fit into a value system?

Pie-on-the-Table Versus Pie-in-the-Sky

Pie-on-the-table is a *functional* value. It is a value which is acted upon. Functional values were the focus of the above discussion. Now we will look at pie-in-the-sky, a label sometimes given to *ideal* values, those values which cannot as yet be put into action.

What we are coming up against here is the problem of *compromise* in the moral life. Politics, for example, is the art of compromise. Better half a cake than no cake at all is the motto. We're going to need a political dimension in our moral lives if we are to survive in a world where evil exists alongside of good. I believe that my taxes are being put to immoral uses. But I pay them anyway and work to elect morally upright officials. I believe that the military system is intrinsically evil. But I register for the draft anyway and apply for conscientious objector status. I believe that the public school is ruinous to my children's morals. But I let them go anyway, and try to counteract the evil at home. By this "political" approach to moral decisions, I make my values functional, livable. I can't do everything, but I compromise and do what I can.

In each one of us there also lives a moral revolutionary who is at odds with this moral politician. This is where *ideal* values come in. There are some things upon which we are simply unwilling to compromise. These are our ideals. We cherish and hold on to them even though they don't fit very well into this nasty world in which we must live. Some people, for example, would believe so profoundly in the evil of the military system that they would not even register in the Selective Service System or pay their income tax to support it. Or take the Amish sect in Pennsylvania. These people will not submit their children to regular public school education, so profoundly do they believe that it would harm the moral life they envisage for their children. By this "revolutionary" approach to moral decision, I treat my values as absolute. I reject compromise, however impractical this might seem.

Carried to an extreme, the revolutionary approach to morality loses all touch with the real world. Such an extremist is the starry-eyed idealist or the religious or political fanatic. His values are absolute, unquestionable and beyond compromise. In the name of morality, he closes his eyes to what *is* and lives in the world of what *ought* to be. But the excessive compromiser in morals is not without his own problems as well. He is a weathervane. No value is sacred. He can be counted on for nothing except his readiness to make a deal. Standing for nothing, he has no vision of what *ought* to be. He is completely submerged in unending compromises with the evil in the world that *is*.

How can we straddle in our moral lives the worlds of *is* and *ought*? How can we be realistic without becoming wishy-washy weathervanes, and at the same time idealistic without being starry eyed or fanatical? How can the sensible moral politician in us live with the idealistic revolutionary? How can we live in the real world, and yet keep our moral ideals alive?

The great American philosopher John Dewey points out how we keep alive those moral ideals which we are unwilling to let go of even though we can't put them into effect. Ritual is what we use.[4] What we can't accomplish practically, we act out ritually. Ritual keeps our ideals alive until the day we can make them a reality. The Western Powers, for example, are unable to risk driving the Russian presence out of Eastern Europe by force of arms. But they wish to maintain the *ideal* of a free Eastern Europe. So each year they declare and celebrate Captive Nations Week. This ritual celebration keeps the ideal alive, though the actual freeing of these nations cannot yet be practically achieved. Most of our national holidays and religious feast days are ritual occasions for reaffirming ideals.

Ku Klux Klanners burn crosses to keep alive their ideal of white supremacy. Women's libbers burn their bras, and decent literature organizations burn "dirty books." All these ritual burnings express ideals that are still awaiting their time. In a pornography-free world where women are equal and whites are supreme, these particular rituals would cease. The respective ideal values would have become functional values.

In Christian liturgics, the faithful sing together and share the sacramental food, thus keeping alive an ideal of brotherhood that they are unable to practice outside the church walls. Christmas gifts and Thanksgiving dinner are pauses in the usual family warfare; these rites keep alive the ideal of family unity in spite of all the actual strife. We have our own personal rituals from wearing a brass bracelet for curing gout to blowing on dice to make the right number come up. In the face of insoluble problems, some people recite prayers, while others get ritually drunk.

Whether or not you agree with the morality of all the above cited ideals or the utility of the particular rituals, the point we make is simply this. The balanced moral life demands that we maintain the tension between functional values and ideal values, between political realism and revolutionary idealism, between is and ought, between compromise and commitment. In the moral life I must tread an uneasy middle path, on the one hand avoiding a dream world by making the necessary compromises, but on the other hand in various ritual ways keeping my ideals alive until I am able to make them part of my everyday life.

What's So Special About "Moral" Values?

This book focuses not on values in general, but specifically on your *moral* values. This can be confusing. Many values get mixed up with morality that don't necessarily have anything to do with it. Consider our most frequently used value words, "bad" and "good," and all the non-moral uses to which we put them. Here are some of the meanings that could be implied by the bad-good distinction.

First, "deviant-conforming": This is the sociological sense of bad-good. Germans in the 1930s who resisted the Nazi anti-Semitic campaign were deviants. The rest were conformists. The government would call the former "bad" and the latter "good." However, were the deviants necessarily immoral and the conformists moral? Hardly.

A second usage is "sin-virtue." This is the religious sense of bad-good. Again, it does not necessarily coincide with immoral-moral. A Roman Catholic woman practicing artificial contraception because another pregnancy would kill her would be called sinful by her pope. Is she necessarily immoral? An Amish parent refusing his child a needed blood transfusion on religious grounds would be called good by his community. Is he necessarily moral? Contrary to common belief, religion and morality don't necessarily go hand in hand. You can have one without the other. More on the relation of religion and morality will follow in the next chapter.

We saw above the usage of good-bad in the sense of effective-ineffective. We might call this the "technological" meaning of value. A good baseball pitcher has an earned run average of 1.9. A bad pitcher has an earned run average of 12. Neither measure of effectiveness necessarily has anything to do with his morality.

Bad-good in a fourth usage is synonymous with odd-proper. Value is assigned to the conventional, disvalue to the unconventional. In the 1960s, for example, hairstyle became the benchmark of who was odd and who was proper. And to be odd was to be bad. For some, Afro haircuts were viewed as a signal for violent revolution. Long-haired auto drivers were stopped and searched by police simply on the basis of the length of their hair. Watergate showed that a crewcut is no assurance of a firm grip on morality. Oddness need not signal immorality, nor does propriety necessarily go hand in hand with morality.

Finally, bad-good is often used to express the distinction between criminal and law-abiding. Is every law-abiding act moral? Does violation of law imply violation of morals? The Nuremberg trials condemned law-abiding Nazis by appealing to a morality higher than law. During the Vietnam era, war-protesters were thrown into jail when they tried to make the same appeal. The relationship of law and morality is a much vexed question in American society and will be a recurrent theme throughout this book.

So values come in many varieties. However, you have to ask—valuable for what? Valuable for getting the job done? This is a practical value (effectiveness). Valuable for being a good citizen? This is a legal value (observance of law). Valuable for getting along with others? This is a social value (conventionality). Valuable for being a God-fearing man? This is a religious value (virtue). Well, what about *moral* value? For what is moral value valuable? We have seen that it does not necessarily mean law-abiding, effective, virtuous, or conforming. What *does* it mean?

An action is *morally* valuable when it is in harmony with what it means for me to be a human being in all that this implies, i.e., in my relationships to myself, to other human beings, to my environment, and if I believe in God or some supernatural dimension to life, then a morally good action would have to take this transcendent into account too. Briefly, a morally good action is one that is faithful to the totality of what it means to be a human being. The morally good man is true to himself in the fullest sense of that phrase. Moral evil, conversely, is infidelity to oneself.

So a legally correct action is *also* moral if it meets this test: Is it true to the totality of what it means to be a human being? Racial discrimination in South Africa may be legal. Does it meet this *moral* test? Infant sacrifices to the deity among the Aztecs may be religiously virtuous. Do they meet this moral test? Accepting a political payoff may be practical. But is it also moral? Does it pass the test of being true to the totality of what it means to be a human being? "I don't know," you rightly answer. "It depends. What exactly do you intend by saying 'the totality of what it means to be a human being'? How do you spell this out?"

The objection is well taken. We have a broad definition of what a moral value is. We're in the right ball park. But in the moral ball park there are many seats. There are many philosophies of man. Tell me your philosophy of man, and I'll tell you the ethics that follows from it, that is in harmony with it. But the root question is: What is your view of man? What does it mean to be faithful to yourself? This is the question that we will be exploring together throughout the rest of the book.

CONCLUSION

This whole enterprise is a waste of time for those who have never had the experience of moral good and moral evil. Such moral defectives, called sociopaths, are fortunately few and far between. So we made the moral experience our starting point and showed three of its

characteristics. The experience of moral obligation (1) is unconditional, (2) involves the whole human being, and (3) is based on one's
philosophy of life. In other words, morality is more than mere expediency, more than mere success, and requires something more than psychology and sociology for its full explanation.

We saw that the moral life revolves around values. It is an illusion to think that you can live in an objective, value-free world. And
action is the acid test of value. But there are some values which we
cherish but which we cannot as yet translate into action. These are
ideal values. They constantly challenge us to reach beyond the world
of functional values, beyond the world of the moral compromises we
have to make in order to survive. The fanatic or ineffective dreamer
has ideals without compromise. The cynical politician has compromise without ideals. The middle road is to live with realism, but to
keep ideals alive in various ritual ways until they can be put into action.

Moral values are in a class apart. They are the test to which the
morally good man submits his other values. Law, convention, conformity, religious virtue, effectiveness—none of these is a guarantee of
morality. What religion considers a virtue can be morally offensive.
The legal act can be a moral evil as can acts which are valued as expedient or conventional. A moral value is one that is in harmony with
what it means to be a human being in all that this implies—in one's
relationships to oneself, to other human beings, to one's environment,
and to the transcendent dimensions of one's life. Each one of us will
spell this out differently. In other words, each one of us has a different philosophy of man. This book will help us reflect on it. The
foundation of ethics lies in your view of what it means to be a human
being.

The formation of such a philosophy of man is a lifelong task. To
grow in morality is to grow as a human being. You really won't be
finished until you're dead! However, you can take a reading of where
you're at now, with a view to fostering this growth in the future.
There are stages to the process of growth, whether you are talking
about physical growth, sexual maturing, or intellectual development.
There are stages to moral growth as well. In the next chapter, we will
call upon psychology to describe these progressive stages of the moral
development of a human being.

TWO:YOUR MORAL IQ

What we call "morals" is simply blind obedience to words of command.

Havelock Ellis

What is moral is what you feel good after and what is immoral is what you feel bad after.

Ernest Hemingway

A moral being is one who is capable of reflecting on his past actions and their motives—of approving of some and disapproving of others.

Charles Darwin[1]

The three descriptions of morality quoted at the head of this chapter seem to contradict each other. Is morality "blind," as Ellis implies, or is it consciously reflective? Is it a matter of "feeling" à la Hemingway, or a matter of judgment as Darwin maintains? All of these descriptions of morality are correct. But each refers to a different level, to a different degree of sophistication and maturity in the moral life. Ellis, we would say (to use the psychological lingo of transactional analysis), is talking about the moral child. This most primitive level of morality is *pre-conventional* morality. Hemingway

21

is speaking at the level of *conventional* morality. This would be the moral parent. And Darwin refers to a mature morality, the *post-conventional* morality of the moral adult.

Psychologist Lawrence Kohlberg[2] has discovered six progressive stages in the development of a fully mature and autonomous moral human being. He shows how each step witnesses a further development in the meaning of "conscience" and in attitudes toward others. And I suggest a parallel development in an ever maturing relation of religion to morals. We will now describe this process. Consider the description of each stage of moral growth. Take your moral IQ. At what level does your moral life now operate? Remember, your moral IQ is not a measure of whether you are good or bad. It is simply an indicator of the *level* of good or bad on which you are operating. A good moral child is better than an evil adult, and no worse than a good adult, if that's the best the child can do.

PRE-CONVENTIONAL MORALITY: THE MORAL CHILD

Pre-conventional morality will become clearer after we see what conventional morality means. The following will suffice for now. At this pre-conventional level, cultural rules are recognized and moral labels are applied. The four-year-old child knows that stealing cookies is "bad" and that using a napkin is "good." He knows that baby sisters should not be hit on the head. However, "good," "bad," and "should" at this level do not refer to the actions in themselves, i.e., to the stealing, the napkin using or the baby bashing. Baby bashing isn't bad because it gives little Ellen a painful bump on the head. No, it's bad because Mom will give me three wallops on the head for every one I gave little Ellen. In other words, morality at the child level refers to the pleasurable or painful consequences of actions. And more primitively, it refers to the sheer physical power of those who announce the rules that are to be obeyed and the labels of good and bad. The child uses moral language which is similar to the adult's: "good," "bad," and "should." But the import is altogether different at this primitive level. Let's take a closer look at pre-conventional morality which comprises two stages: first, the punishment-obedience orientation, and second, the instrumental-relativist orientation.

Stage One: Punishment-Obedience Orientation

Fear of punishment, and fear of punishment alone, is the operative motivation at the first level of moral action. The question is not whether this action is good or bad in itself. The question is rather: If I do this, will I "get it"? But the moral child is not all that conscious of such considerations at this stage. The fear of punishment mechanism operates blindly, automatically, unconsciously. He knows, or better, he *feels:* "If I do this, boy, will I get it!" This is morality on the level of taboo. Stage one morality is operating in the intent, wide-eyed, guilty expression of the child who is alone in the back yard playing with matches, in the nameless fear of retribution experienced by the adolescent after masturbating, and in the grown-up driver who goes through a red light on a deserted road at 3:00 a.m. and casts a guilty look over his shoulder, half expecting a cop to materialize out of nowhere.

Stage one morality is not without its values. It gets the lifelong moral enterprise off and running for the child. The moral taboos are useful too. It's a good thing for the child to feel inhibited about playing with matches even before he is able to comprehend the reasons why. Even for grown-ups, it helps to be automatically programmed to drive safely rather than consciously and rationally weighing the pros and cons of every stop sign. That taboo against running a red light on a deserted road, irrational though it may be, is not all bad. Grown-ups as well as children in many areas of moral life operate on stage one morality: the punishment-obedience orientation.

This moral child (which occasionally takes over in grown-ups) focuses directly on the taboo against disobedience and the fear of punishment in themselves. Punishment is not seen as supporting an underlying moral order. In the above cited examples, fire prevention, mature sexuality, and traffic safety are not the center of moral consideration. No, it's the punishment: "My mother would kill me for playing with matches," "God's going to get me for masturbating," or, "I bet there's a cop hidden in the bushes." The authority figures— mother, God, and policeman —are feared and obeyed for their own sake, simply because they are authorities. *What* they command or the moral order that they support is irrelevant. The taboo, the authority, the punishment are enough. That's all that matters.

"Motive," "conscience," "love," "religion"—the list of moral categories could go on—are all colored by this peculiar tint of stage one moral eyeglasses. The moral child obeys, not because it's the intelligent thing to do, not because it's good for him or good for you; no, the motive of his moral life is to avoid punishment. "Conscience" also has a particular stage one meaning. In general, conscience is the faculty or power by which we tell moral right from moral wrong. This power in stage one is not a rational consideration of the action in itself. It's not even a weighing of the pain of punishment against the benefits of disobedience: This would be too rational. No, conscience here prompts obedience on the basis of a blind, automatic, irrational fear of punishment.

The same thing happens in the case of love. By "love" we'll refer in the broadest possible sense to all those actions and attitudes toward others that are in any way positive. Obedience, then, is a kind of love for the moral child. But mother is not obeyed because she is good in herself or even because she is useful to the child. Mother is obeyed because she has clout. The moral life in stage one is strictly a power game. My love (i.e., my respect and obedience) of other people is strictly in proportion to the wattage of the thunderbolts that they are ready to hurl when their taboos are violated. In stage one religion, God has infinite wattage (enough to fire up everlasting infernal fires). Religion is often used at this primitive level to back up morality with an infinite divine clout. God is not primarily a loving Father or even a law giver or rewarder. He is the angry, vengeful punisher. If evildoers don't get it in this life, he'll see to it that they get it in the next.

Again, stage one morality is not confined to children. It includes those grown-ups who say that without a punisher God, morality would be impossible; that if God did not exist, there would be no reason for being morally good. It includes those grown-ups who blindly act and react to authority automatically in terms of fear and power. Doubtless all of us, whatever our chronological age, have pockets of our moral lives that are guided by this pre-conventional morality of the moral child. Stage two morality, even though it remains on the pre-conventional level, is an advance over this punishment-obedience orientation.

Stage Two: Instrumental-Relativist Orientation

This is still the moral child in action, but morality at this second stage, according to Kohlberg's analysis, becomes more rational, less blind. The aim is to maximize pleasure and minimize pain. Morality is "instrumental" and "relative" to this goal. It's a "you scratch my back and I'll scratch yours" morality. Reciprocity and fairness on this basic pragmatic level are all important. This is the kind of razor-sharp justice that rules in the children's playground, or at the dinner table when the pie is being sliced up and divided. "It's not fair!" is stage two's ultimate moral appeal. Or "her slice is bigger than mine!" The world is a marketplace for satisfying my needs. There is a moral calculus ever at work—how to maximize satisfaction and mini-mize frustration. Jeremy Bentham's utilitarian ethics might be con-sidered a grown-up version of stage two morality, where moral good is defined as the greatest happiness for the greatest number of people.

This is an advance over stage one. Actions are no longer blindly labeled good or bad, but they are evaluated in their own right. The value sought is instrumental: "What will this action do for me?" Punishment is still a factor. But punishment no longer leads to blind conformity. It becomes part of the calculus. For example, eight-year-old Bobby sees his older brother fooling with his Dad's best camera and breaking it. His Dad thinks he, Bobby, did it. Moral question: Should Bobby squeal? Stage two moral calculus: "Who will beat me up worse, my older brother if I squeal or my Dad if I don't?" Though morality at this stage is still selfishly utilitarian, it represents a growth of rationality and freedom. The child is no longer a victim of blind taboos. His calculation of the benefits of various courses of ac-tion frees him from this kind of slavery. By acquiring a sense of freedom and learning to use his head in moral matters, he is readying himself for that higher level of moral living which we call conven-tional morality.

Stage two, however, is still definitely pre-conventional. True, there is fairness and reciprocity. There is a kind of "justice." But the moral vision goes no further than the individual and his immediate pragmatic needs. This is not justice for its own sake. Nor are the "give and take" activities motivated by a sense of loyalty or of grati-tude. No, the reciprocity here is strictly of the calculating variety. People are not valued in themselves. They are there to be manipu-lated. I give in order to get. The con-man or the cynical advertiser or politician is liable to live much of his moral life with this narrow in-strumental-relativist orientation. Although you are grown-up, are there areas of your moral life where the moral child of stage two remains operative?

"Conscience" now is no longer an irrational faculty that blindly whispers "good good" or "bad bad" in your ear when you are con-fronted with a moral decision. The instrumentalist conscience engages in a rational calculus. Guilt feelings are no longer the overriding con-sideration. Punishment is viewed pragmatically along with the other pleasurable and painful consequences of a moral decision. To cite a trivial example, I may calculate that a parking fine is well worth the convenience of stationing my car near my place of work. Where stage one blindly fears all encounters with the law, stage two inquires how the law will affect my sum of pleasure and pain. This is moral progress in that conscience is more rational, but it remains the conscience of the child in that it is completely egotistical and self-serving.

The meaning of "love" follows suit. Other people are viewed as people and not merely as wielders of clout. However, the view is manipulative. Love depends on the answer to the question: What have you done for me lately? "Mommy, I'm sorry you're sick. I love you and want you to get well, because if you don't, who's going to cook my meals for me?" Gratitude for what Mommy has done in the past does not enter the picture, nor do her prerogatives as a human being in her own right.

At stage two, religion can still be used to back up morality. This level of religion remains magical but with a difference from stage one. No longer is it a question of blindly doing and undoing taboos. God is viewed as someone to be calculatingly manipulated just as people are. Moral bargains are struck with God. "I'll cut out smoking, if you see that I get a pay raise." "If I go to church every Sunday, you'd better see that my son comes home safely from the war." As with love of people, so the love of God will depend on how well he comes through for me. At this level of religious morality, that mother whose son did not come home safely from the war is liable to abandon religion altogether.

CONVENTIONAL MORALITY: THE MORAL PARENT

We have seen that however primitive it might be, this instrumentalist morality represented an advance over the punishment-obedience orientation of stage one. But now we make a quantum leap to a new level in the psychology of moral development. This is to the level of the much maligned "conventional morality." Kohlberg finds here a radical shift in focus away from the egocentric moral child outward toward the expectations of society. To adapt quite loosely the metaphor used by transactional analysis, what is operative here is the morality no longer of the child but of the *parent*. We each carry around with us an aspect of our personality (our parent) which embodies everything expected of us as devoted family members, good citizens, and as loyal participants in the groups to which we belong. The sum of these laws, social taboos, and expectations we call conventional morality. It is fashionable in some circles to criticize conventional morality as "bourgeois" and petty for great-hearted souls. True, it is not the last word in morality. Conventional moral principles can be evaluated from a higher vantage point, as we will see. But criticism of conventional morality is not always as lofty as it seems. It is easier for the egocentric child to take potshots at it than to live up to its relatively altruistic demands. It is no easy morality that exacts devoted loyalty to one's family and unremitting support of one's nation. Devotion to the group rather than selfish preoccupations now occupies the center of moral concern. Progress in the moral life at the conventional level encompasses two stages: first, the interpersonal concordance orientation, and secondly, the law and order orientation.

Stage Three: Interpersonal Concordance Orientation

The approval of others who are close to me is the all-important motive at this stage. This is the morality of the "good little boy" and the "nice girl." Parental morality has been successfully incorporated into their own behavior. This parent who lives within them provides a set of maxims to guide them in moral decision-making. "Chew with your mouth closed." "Come when your mother calls." "Wash the tub after you take a bath." "Don't cross the street in the middle of the block." "All Jews are cheats." "Never talk to strangers." "Children should be seen and not heard." "Never a lender or a debtor be." The existence of this moral parent is not a matter of chronological age. Just as the pre-conventional moral child was seen to exist in grown-ups as well as children, so the conventional moral parent is part of the makeup of children as well as grown-ups. The eight-year-old is acting like a good little boy when he washes the tub after taking a bath. You may find this same person at the age of sixty religiously washing the tub. His physical parents are long since dead, but the moral parent within him lives on.

Stage three morality is explicitly directed toward helping and pleasing others. The moral child was a slave to his fears (stage one) and to his selfish pleasure (stage two). Conventional morality is a step toward freedom from these enslavements. In spite of fear, in spite of inconvenience or pain to myself, I do the "right thing." And the right thing is defined for me by the groups to which I belong, especially, at this stage, the family. I know what they expect. I desire and need their approval. I conform and thereby win the honor that comes with being a loyal member. No longer are my egotistical fears and desires the center of the universe. I have learned that others exist in their own right, and I bend my will to please them. And this is no blind and fearful conformity. I understand the importance of my actions for the group. I see the group and the order maintained by the group as valuable in themselves. And so I support it regardless of the inconvenient consequences to myself. This altruism puts conventional morality miles ahead of the pre-conventional variety, at least if your philosophy of man recognizes that others besides yourself have a value and worth in their own right.

Moral categories at stage three take on a social orientation. The group or society to which I belong lets me know by its approval or disapproval what is right and what is wrong. Thus conscience is other-oriented. Fear of disapproval by the group motivates me to live up to its expectations. My moral identity is no longer wrapped up in myself, but is inextricably entwined with others. Love is no longer the manipulative relationship of stage two. Mommy, for example, is valued as a person in her own right and not merely because she gets the meals out on time. There is gratitude for what she has done in the past and not just for what she has done lately. Love at this stage also involves loyalty. In fact, loyalty is valued more highly by the group than the instrumental efficiency of stage two. This is expressed in attitudes of approval such as "he means well," "she's nice." At stage two you are loved if you produce, if you come through. Here, you are loved if you stick with the group, are a good team player, or a loyal member of the family.

Conventional morality commonly calls upon religion to back up its expectations. The rules and standards of the group get assimilated to the "will of God." The result is that when you don't live up to the expectations of your relatives or your neighbors, you are flaunting not merely the family or the neighborhood, but the divinity itself. It is God's will and not merely a family idiosyncracy that drinking is not tolerated in your home. It is no mere social convention but God's will that couples not cohabit without benefit of wedlock. In other words, God becomes the most respected member of the group in question and the symbol of all its moral expectations. Love and loyalty to the group are synonymous with love and loyalty to God. Reject one and you reject the other.

The big problem with conventional morality, of course, both at this stage and the next, is its inability to handle conflict of loyalties. A student wishes to invite a racially mixed couple to a party at his parents' home, much to their horror. Family loyalty confronts peer group loyalty. Two sets of conventions come into conflict. Which group should the student honor? Only a move to the level of post-conventional morality can adequately handle this question.

Conventional morality, however, can deal in a limited way with such conflicts. Stage three morality remains very parochial. The conventions and the social controls are administered personally by people I somehow know face to face. In other words, the groups involved are relatively intimate: family, neighborhood, peers, clubs, fellow-workers. And since one person can belong to many groups, conflicts easily arise. There is, however, a wider social structure that includes all these subgroups. This society has a set of fixed impersonal standards by which the lower stage conventions can be judged. We are talking about the next stage of moral growth, the law and order orientation. Though we remain at the conventional level, Kohlberg's next stage represents a real advance over stage three in freedom, rationality, and universality.

Stage Four: Law and Order Orientation

When moral conventions come into conflict, it's becoming a practice as American as apple pie to look automatically to the courts and the law for settlement. The impersonal authority of the law takes precedence over the personal loyalties of stage three. Morality becomes again more sophisticated. A sense of duty arises that transcends personal feelings. The need for maintaining social order in the state is recognized, and to this end the authority of the law is paid unswerving respect. Without the framework of this wider social order, clearly the life of the subgroups (family, neighborhood, etc.) would be threatened. The stage four law and order orientation is based upon the recognition of these wider and more universal social concerns.

In popular political parlance, "law and order" has been disparaged as a synonym for racial oppression, suppression of individual liberties, and an ultra-strong police force. This caricature should not blind us to the genuine moral advance represented by the law and order orientation that we are describing here. At stage four the individual is able to extend his moral vision beyond the narrow confines of the groups in which he is accustomed to move. He sees the need for law even where the law does not touch him personally. He respects the rights of people whom he doesn't know and wouldn't even want to know. And to these ends he recognizes and performs his moral duty even at the cost of personal feelings and narrower loyalties. In fact, "duty" is the watchword of stage four morality.

Conscience, love, religion all take on more universal and rational meaning. Conscience, the indicator of moral right and wrong, is still socially oriented. But the anticipated approval and disapproval which guides my moral decisions is now formalized in the law and institutionalized in the legal process. The society toward which I look for approval as a man of duty extends beyond the informal subgroups of family, peers, and neighborhood. It embraces all those who ascribe to the law and to the rights and duties that flow therefrom. The law and order orientation in this sense is a liberation from the more confining parochial morality of stage three. I become able to judge and act upon moral issues that transcend the informal emotional bonds of family and friends.

This is not to say, however, that duty replaces love. Love becomes less sentimental and more rational. My feelings are less enslaved to the fear of what others may think. My love is shown by a concern for the true good of others, respect for their rights, and fidelity to the duties I owe them. For example, the conventional morality of my family at stage three might absolutely prohibit interracial dating or even interracial neighborhoods. But faced with these situations at stage four, familial morality does not have the last word. My loving concern extends beyond the family, and my moral decisions will consider the rights and welfare of this wider society as well as of my family. It's not so much how others feel about me that causes guilt. Rather, I would feel guilty for doing concrete harm to others by violating their rights as human beings. In a word, from being informal and sentimental at stage three, now, according to Kohlberg, my love becomes more rational, objective and realistic. It is based less on fear of disapproval than on fear of doing harm.

I suggest that this law and order orientation is very prone to co-opt the services of God as a kind of supercop. Breakdown of religion and breakdown of law become associated with each other. And God-fearing and law-abiding tend to become synonymous. The hearthstone deity of stage three becomes the tribal God in stage four. "For God and country" becomes the slogan. The laws of the nation become the laws of heaven, and God is the foremost citizen. And all lawbreakers, be they murderers or marijuana smokers, abortionists, or conscientious objectors, become not merely criminals but sinners.

This co-opting of religion in the service of law points up a parochial strain even in stage four morality for all its rationality and universality. The universality tends to stop at the nation's boundaries. So law and order morality remains conventional, i.e., dependent upon a particular group for its validity. The group here is primarily the nation. It is only through a final quantum leap to post-conventional morality that this limitation is overcome. Only at the autonomous principled level of post-conventional morality does morality become truly universal.

POST-CONVENTIONAL MORALITY:
THE MORAL ADULT

As long as moral rules are relative to certain groups—Americans, Baptists, the Fenwick family, Maoists, South Chicagoans, French Canadians, Anglicans—morality remains conventional. It lacks complete universality. It is valid only on the authority of these groups and applies only to their members. Post-conventional morality is a shift to moral values and principles whose validity is independent of particular groups or of membership in particular societies. From the moral parent who follows out the precepts of his society, we shift to the moral adult who autonomously evaluates his society's precepts and decides whether indeed they should be followed out. The shift is away from the group and back to the individual, but not to the egotistical moral child of level one. The child knows nothing of moral conventions; the adult knows them all too well. For the child to submit to conventional morality is progress; for the adult to submit is regression. The child is selfish, and conventions bring him out of himself to recognition of the group; the adult is autonomous, and slavery to convention would suck him back into the groups which he is transcending. The child is not yet social; the adult is transsocial. The adult's concern for others knows no group limits or social boundaries. But precisely because no one group holds his moral allegiance, he is autonomous and alone in his moral decisions.

Again, Kohlberg distinguishes two stages in this progress toward moral autonomy: first, the social contact rational orientation, and secondly, the universal ethical principle orientation.

Stage Five: Social Contract Rational Orientation

It has been said that pro football, Thanksgiving Day, the World Series, and Mother's Day are rites of the official American civil religion. In the same vein we can say that stage five morality represents the official American civil morality. This is *par excellence* the morality of a pluralistic society. It is a formula for consensus. The focus is more on the *method* of arriving at agreement and less on the actual content of the agreement. No one group, no set of conventions is sacred. A moral consensus in a pluralistic society must rely on compromise. Tolerance is the cardinal virtue. Reason is the guiding norm. Peaceful social cooperation among conflicting groups is the goal. Such "social contracts" are arrived at in legislative chambers, in court decisions, in town hall meetings, neighborhood pow-wows, written agreements, and handshakes. The important thing is not that all should agree, but that all should live together in peace.

Gone are the rigidly held conventions of stage four. While law is to be obeyed, it is not sacred. It is not meant to enshrine the morality of any particular group. Stage four moralists will fight to have their particular conventions legalized. They will fight to codify their particular views on abortion, pornography, pot, prayer, and divorce. The stage five moralist is aware of the relative nature of moral conventions. Laws can be changed. They should be changed when they cater to parochial special interests over the common pluralistic good. Rational considerations of social utility are paramount. What the laws *are* is less important than what they *do*. Stage five morality is a declaration of independence from the tyranny of convention. Reason replaces group loyalty in the driver's seat.

Group-centered morality demands faith. Consensus morality appeals to reason. Right and wrong are not feelings but judgments about social utility. Conscience is now a rational guide of action. The approval of others for conforming to their expectations and doing my duty is not what motivates me. True, I seek the respect of others. But I seek respect as an equal, as a man of reason, and therefore as someone to be reckoned with although not necessarily agreed with. Perhaps more importantly, I am motivated by self-respect. My rational conscience would find it hard to live with irrational, inconsistent, and purposeless behavior.

My love now takes on an equally rational dimension. It knows no group limits or national boundaries. The community in which my moral life now moves is the community of reason. This community is potentially as wide as the human race itself, qualifying therefore as a truly universal community. My love at stage five is able to respect every human being however different, peculiar, or alien he may appear to my customary moral way of living. It was on this basis that the Nuremberg trials, for example, appealed to a law of mankind that took precedence over any merely national morality. Thus post-conventional morality can judge immoral what was perfectly moral at the conventional level.

If there is a religious dimension to moral living at this stage, I suggest that it, too, would be characterized by universality and rationality. It might take on the accents, for example, of "secular

Christianity," or carry placards that proclaim: "Jesus is reality." It knows no set of conventions that enjoy peculiar divine backing. Even in the churches, then, at this stage the responsibility for finding moral rules and answers is shifted to men working, reasoning, and compromising together. Reality with its problems is there as a gift of God. Human reason is also there as a gift. And then, there is no further divine intervention except an implied exhortation: "Go to it with honesty, love, and mutual respect, and good luck!" Mankind's "coming of age" as proclaimed by Bonhoeffer is congenial to the moral maturity of stage five.

Stage Six: Universal Ethical-Principle Orientation

In the analysis by psychologist Lawrence Kohlberg which we have been following, moral development culminates in the universal ethical-principle orientation. Here the movement toward maturity and responsibility begun in stage five reaches its fulfillment in the complete moral adult—the moral need to maintain one's own self-respect. Upholding one's self-chosen moral principles becomes more important than achieving rational moral compromise. I am completely my own man in moral matters ready to stand alone if need be for what I believe.

My conscience asks only one question: Am I being true to myself? I fear self-condemnation more than condemnation by any other man. My decisions are based not on the concrete moral rules of conventional morality, or on the rational compromises of stage five, but on abstract universal principles by which I have chosen to live. At stage six, my heart may well have reasons of which the mind knows not. Where the faith underlying conventional morality may be called prerational, the faith in one's moral sense at stage six is transrational. We will explore this high moral ideal further in the final chapter. Suffice it to say now that this faith that comes with maturity underlies the moral self-assurance of the saints, prophets, and great moral leaders. For example, in America during the 1960s, both Lyndon Baines Johnson and Martin Luther King had a mature moral concern for racial equality. Would, perhaps, Johnson's approach represent the rational ethic of stage five? And did King possess the prophetic vision that accompanies the complete moral autonomy of stage six?

PERSONAL OBSERVATIONS

Clearly the realities of moral growth are much more complicated than the six steps just neatly outlined, beginning with the punishment-obedience orientation of the moral child and culminating in the principled autonomy of the full-fledged moral adult. Different facets of my moral life develop at different rates. My sexual ethics, for example, could remain arrested at the taboo level of the child, while my business ethics are conducted at a level that is perfectly mature. The schema simply intends to spell out concretely what moral progress looks like. Compare your behavior to the behavioral signals of pre-conventional morality, as well as to conventional and post-conventional morality. Where do your moral decisions lie along this scale? In what areas do you surrender to your blind guilt feelings? In what matters do you let custom and law be your guide? For what decisions do you take the full responsibility on your own shoulders regardless of the approval or disapproval of others? The answers to these questions are indicators of your moral IQ, not of your moral worth. They hint at where you are at now and suggest a direction for growth.

Of course, such a scale of moral progress relies upon certain assumptions about a philosophy of man, about what it means to be a human being. Growth is measured in terms of increased rationality, progress in freedom, and the ability to love more and more universally. These themes will be touched upon from different viewpoints in the following chapters. Some philosophers will dispute the rationality of man. For others, freedom is an illusion, and love is impossible. Such philosophers would have radically different conceptions about the measure of moral growth from the one outlined above.

Whatever one's philosophy is, it must certainly be admitted that the moral life is something less than an unbridled march toward freedom and autonomy. Karl Marx is eloquent on the economic barriers to moral freedom. There is no need to read Marx; consult your bankbook and your credit rating. Sociologist Durkheim sees society as erecting the moral prison walls within which each of us is doomed to serve a life sentence. There is no need to read Durkheim. Just try to deviate from what your parents or your neighbors consider to be the sign of a morally good man, and see how far you get. Sociology, economics, and anthropology describe in detail the moral fences that hem us in. The theme, then, of the next chapter is "Morality as Prison." We will hear sociologists Peter Berger and Thomas Luckmann tell how these prison walls are built. Then contemporary Marxist Herbert Marcuse will show how these prison walls are rendered invisible. And anthropologist Mary Douglas will point out some factors which determine how high or low these walls remain. The first step to freedom is to learn the nature of our slavery. As Richard Tawney has pointed out: "Slavery will work—as long as the slaves will let it."[3]

THREE:MORALITY AS PRISON

Man is born free; and everywhere he is in chains. One thinks himself the master of others, and still remains a greater slave than they.

Jean Jacques Rousseau

The method of production of the material things of life generally determines the social, political and spiritual currents of life.

Karl Marx

Men would not live long in society were they not the dupes of each other.

Francois de la Rochefoucauld

"All the world's a stage," said Shakespeare. "All the world's a prison," suggest the philosophers quoted at the head of this chapter. Morality is the tyrant that casts us into this prison. Sometimes we recognize the jailer. Sometimes we don't. The adolescent rebelling against parental strictures knows that from which he's trying to escape. So does the revolutionary who rises up against unjust laws. When something human is trying to grow inside of me, it bursts the bonds of any morality that would try to hold it in. In the last chapter we described this thrust beyond conventions to a post-conventional

35

morality where my philosophy of man is what counts, i.e., where I take my stand on what it means for me to be a human being.

It is more dangerous to my budding humanity when I don't recognize the moral jailer. This is the danger cited above by Rousseau, Marx, and de la Rochefoucauld. We think we're free, says Rousseau, while society has us in its chains. The first section of this chapter, "Imprisoned by Your Neighbor's Propaganda," describes these chains. We think that we are masters of our moral lives, says Marx, whereas in truth we are cogs in the economic machine. Section two, "Imprisoned by Economic Propaganda," explores this Marxist theme. Our very philosophy of man, suggests de la Rochefoucauld, rests on a delusion. Section three, "Imprisoned by Your Own Propaganda," exposes this self-delusion.

IMPRISONED BY YOUR NEIGHBOR'S PROPAGANDA:
BERGER AND LUCKMANN

"Leave your common sense at the door!" is what theologian Gustav Weigel used to tell his students on the first day of class. This admonition confirmed all their man-in-the-street suspicions against academic ivory-towerism. But it was good advice. One man's common sense is another man's poison—as is one man's meat. In America it is only common sense to keep meat refrigerated until you are ready to cook and eat it. In parts of Micronesia it is common sense to bury meat until it rots and then dig it up and eat it—a great delicacy. Cows show no such varied ingenuity in the preparation of food. They swallow hay and chew their cuds all over the world. And there's no *Kama Sutra* written for the canine species. Dogs everywhere do it one way only—*a tergo*. In sociological terms, where other animals are species-specific, humans are "world-open." Dogs and cows express their instincts in biologically fixed ways. But the human expression of instincts is flexible, "open," and subject to socio-cultural determination.

Sociology of Knowledge

Now a man of "common sense" won't realize how open his world really is, or could be. He tends to freeze his particular way of doing things into "natural laws," thus becoming as rigid as the horses and the cows. "My way is the right way, the only way, the moral thing to do." Now when the missionaries came to Hawaii and found the natives doing it *a tergo*, their reforms were instant and uncompromising: henceforth man-on-top—for such is common sense back in New England. An unflattering synonym for common sense is *shared prejudice*. Get enough people to assure each other that a particular way of looking at things—a particular world-view—is true, and for them it becomes more real, true and everlasting than the stars in heaven. Sociologist Peter Berger puts it this way: "Every *Weltanschauung* (i.e., world-view) is a conspiracy."[1] What you believe as common sense, you believe only because you are the willing victim of a conspiracy. In a word, you are imprisoned by your neighbor's propaganda. Such is the wry sociological perspective on the morals game. Let's consider it.

Propaganda, to be effective, must not be recognized as such. And this is the case with common sense. Nothing is further from being considered as propaganda. Rather, common sense stands for what's real, for "what everybody knows to be true." In other words, this common sense world is completely taken for granted. It doesn't enter my mind to question common sense. This taken for granted world is by definition made up of those values and realities that are beyond question. If they were subject to question, they wouldn't be common sense. This taken for granted value and reality system is my "inclusive world." It is my universe. It sets the standard by which I test all my sub-worlds, my "included worlds." Things are more or less real and true depending upon how closely they measure up to this taken for granted world.

In the witch doctor world of deep Africa, the overarching taken for granted reality is made up of invisible spirits and powers, some beneficent and others deadly, to be invoked or appeased. No mere Western medicine can save a man who believes that he lies under the curse of these powers. Bring him to a Western type hospital, and he will die. Bring him to a witch doctor, and he might live. The power of Western medicine pales into unreality in an inclusive world where these invisible forces are the standard of what is most real and most true. An unrecognized conspiracy keeps this particular variety of common sense intact. "Everybody knows" who the good witch doctors are and who the evil ones are. "Everybody knows" which amulets are the most powerful against malevolent spirits. The signs of being under a curse and the dangers of ignoring these signs are part of the conventional wisdom. Certain types of dreams must be heeded as more real and more true than the assurances of Western brand scientific common sense. It is hard to live intimately in a witchcraft so-

ciety without being sucked, almost against one's will, into that particular conspiracy. This is the reason behind the common phenomenon
of "going native." Peter Berger has a picturesque way of stating this
conspiracy theory of reality and truth. "You choose your beliefs," he
says, "by choosing your playmates." What counts for real depends
upon what game you are playing. And what game you are playing
depends upon who your playmates are, i.e., upon what the inclusive
world is of the society in which you live. Parents everywhere instinc-
tively realize the force of this sociological fact. That's why they try to
protect their children from "bad companions." New companions
mean a new definition of reality. LSD experiences, for example, in
the parental inclusive world are "hallucinations." But in a spaced out
culture such experiences are revered as putting one in touch with the
ultimate oneness and reality of the universe. There are two opposing
inclusive worlds here, two versions of common sense. Each considers
its own taken for granted universe as unassailable, and on these
grounds judges the other as less real, good, and true. Each *Weltanschauung* is supported by an unrecognized conspiracy.

Change the conspirators, and reality itself changes. Transport
the witch doctor to a fashionable New York cocktail party if you
would loosen the hold over him of his good and evil spirits. Leave
him long enough in this new-found social circle, and he will come to
marvel at his former "superstition" and wonder that his fellow tribes-
men once believed him to be specially endowed. And Indian students
in American universities from orthodox Hindu families before long
will find themselves eating cow meat. And Peace Corps volunteers to
Latin America soon renounce their former American "superstitious"
belief in tight time schedules and ruthless competition. Transport
American doctors to Chinese hospitals and acupuncture becomes
transformed from a quasi-magical, primitive medical practice into a
legitimate therapeutic procedure. Change the conspirators and reality
itself changes. What counts for real is a value judgment. So we can
say, change your playmates and you change your values.[2]

The Social Construction of Moral Reality

In the above dramatic examples, the social impact on value beliefs is obvious. But for most of us, our value systems are not so
dramatically challenged. We keep basically the same playmates
throughout most of our lives. Their influence on us is less obvious but
just as forceful. They lay down the rules of the game by which we

decide what is real and true and morally good or bad. It's almost impossible to realize upon what a shaky foundation my own common sense rests. A Christian feels that he can understand the precarious nature of Hindu beliefs. They conflict so much with his own common sense. But the opposite is also true. The Hindu views the Christian denial of reincarnation as the depth of ignorance. How can a man presume to plumb the depths of liberated wisdom in only one lifetime?

Our society, like most others, makes it almost impossible to ask questions that would subvert "common sense." We pretend now and then to ask such ultimate subversive questions, but we don't really believe them. It has been said that philosophers more than most people enjoy this game of pretend. This chapter, perhaps, is a good example. We question your most basic values. But when you close the book, you easily return to the taken for granted everyday world again. It's like dreaming. Common sense is suspended and the rules of reality are overturned. It can be a nightmare. But the alarm clock happily returns me to my safe, established universe again.

Art is another feeble attempt to subvert common sense values. We go to the theatre and willingly suspend our ordinary beliefs. We cheer the clever swindler, boo at the police, and enjoy spectacular violence. However, once out again on the crowded sidewalks of reality, the swindler is no friend, the policeman is a helper, and the violent murder is once more a tragedy. Philosophy, dreams and art are subworlds in the all-embracing world of common sense normalcy. These "included" worlds temporarily put into question the taken for granted assumptions of the inclusive world. But the latter almost always wins. It is beyond question because it is the basis upon which all questions are decided.

Birth, puberty, marriage, and most of all death, are the experiences that can shake to its foundations the taken for granted common sense world. Because these marginal experiences are most dangerous to our beliefs, we devise ways to exorcise their subversive sting. Consider death, the most traumatic of these experiences. The brute fact of death has the power to call into question everything I've ever lived for, anything I've ever loved or considered to be true or good or beautiful. Complacent everyday attitudes threaten to crumble in the face of death. We have two ways of bringing this marginal experience into the pale of normalcy: ritual and denial. In these two ways, we bring death into our inclusive world and thus protect our common sense values.

First, ritual. The funeral rites give us ordinary everyday things to consciously occupy us while we unconsciously adjust to the traumatic shock. We make arrangements with the undertaker, hold the wake, buy mourning clothes, take part in prayer and religious ceremony, reassure ourselves of another eternal life, tell each other that life must go on, etc. This last is probably the most significant. "Life must go on." In other words, we can't let death shatter our everyday world. We dare not let death reveal to us the senseless absurdity and precarious reality of all that we hold dear. "Life must go on." Thus ritual exorcises the subversive power of death and submits it to our normal world.

Modern America, unlike most societies, deals with death by denial, as well as by ritual. Death raises such subversive questions as: What is the purpose of life? Why must I die? Who am I? Whence and whither am I? Alongside of such questions, what does it matter how much beef has gone up in price or who's sleeping with the girl next door? The preacher can raise the big questions for an hour on Sundays, but he doesn't really touch us. On the way out of the church to the parking lot, food prices and bedroom gossip take over again. Such is the power over us of the everyday common sense world. We hide our old people. We deny death. We worship the young. And so life goes on in unquestioned complacency.

From the sociological standpoint we have been adopting, this book may be asking the impossible of you. It challenges you to reflect on and question your most taken for granted values. It challenges you *not* to be taken in by your neighbor's propaganda, but to give yourself a dose of culture-shock. Can you see yourself and your values as they would look to an alien who just dropped in from another planet? This alien visitor doesn't know what "everybody knows." He's unfamiliar with your playmates and their particular conspiracies. When he sees the "real" world that so earnestly occupies you, he may shake his head and murmur "far out!" Your most cherished moral values could shock him. Lacking the social support of your conspiracy, he might not realize, for example, what a great and noble thing it is to slaughter for one's fatherland in time of war.

From time to time, the sub-worlds of dreams, of art, of philosophy, and of marginal experiences like death try to seduce us from our inclusive world. But we remain firmly in the grip of our neighbor's propaganda. Travel (either by social mobility or by a geographical move) into new societies with new playmates can loosen this grip. Of course, the moment of my death will be the complete liberation. How does the common sense world look when viewed from my coffin? That man is truly free who lives each moment as if it were his last. But how many such free persons walk among us?

IMPRISONED BY ECONOMIC PROPAGANDA: MARCUSE

Technological Rationality

Sociology, as we have just seen, paints a rather dismal picture of how hard it is to take a good critical look at our taken for granted value system. Society, it seems, weaves a value trap in which we are inevitably enmeshed. Let's now examine this value trap from another point of view. The more we know about its construction, the better chance we have of springing loose from it. We'll get the best information from our enemies rather than from our friends. After all, our friends are caught in the same trap: They are "co-conspirators." So we turn now to a Marxist critique of the philosophy of man, and therefore of the ethics, fostered by American society. Modern day Marxist Herbert Marcuse has given the most eloquent diagnosis of how the economic power structure in America enslaves our thoughts, actions and moral values.[3] So put on a Marxist uniform and consider an enslavement which is more devastating than the social determinisms pointed out in the previous section. The propaganda here carries economic clout. You'd better believe it if you want to eat.

First, our very thought processes are corrupted by *operational* thinking. Operational thinking locks us into our inclusive world and makes it impossible to be self-critical about our values. Briefly, operational thinking says this: "You are what you do." Things are defined by the way they operate. A "hammer" is whatever bangs nails into wood or pulls them loose. A "free election" is secretly voting for one of the candidates of the major political parties listed on the ballot. A "baby" is an eating, sleeping, screaming, excreting organism. In other words, if you want to know what something is, look at what it does.

So what's wrong with operational thinking? It does away with our ideals—that's what's wrong, says Marcuse. It locks us into the *status quo*. It blocks out alternatives. It reduces us. It says, you are *nothing but* what you do. When a mother looks at her baby, doesn't she see something more than "an eating, screaming, excreting organism"? Of course. She sees a possible doctor, lawyer, or president. Operational thinking blocks out the ideal person that the baby can become. When "free election" is defined as the process of voting for one of the major party candidates on the ballot, again we're locked into the *status quo*. We don't even consider alternative possibilities that could bring greater freedom than our present process of choosing from among nearly identical candidates. This same operational thinking blinds us when we define a "hammer" by the things that the hammer on your shelf can do. It keeps us from trying to create an "ideal" hammer, one, for example, that could drive in nails without banging or noise. Operational thinking makes moral pygmies of us. It keeps us so focused on what is, that we never raise our eyes to what ideally might be.

Operational thinking is enslaved thinking. This is no mere philosophical quibble over words. We have become literally slaves to the economic power structure, says Marcuse. But we don't realize it. We actually think that we are free. This type of thinking has pacified us, resigned us to our slavery. So each workday we obediently go through our paces as slaves in the "free enterprise" system, cogs in the industrial machine. It never occurs to us that it is a strange kind of freedom that forces us to live, sleep, structure our hours and days, make purchases, and pay taxes all according to the demands of the economy. Our lives are not our own. And if we fail to meet these demands, the penalty is poverty, hunger, disease, and ostracism from the mainstream of social life. In our "free" society, a man without a job is less than a man and treated accordingly. It goes even further. Our "free" economy suspects a man without financial credit and a man who is not in debt. The hard-working, decent, safe, approved citizen is one who has bartered away his future until he is literally owned by his creditors. An industry will not hire the single man who has no strings attached in preference to the heavily mortgaged family man. The latter they can own. The tragedy is not so much that this is the case. The tragedy is that we accept it as inevitable.

Operational thinking makes this possible. What's good for the economy is good for the individual. We never dream of questioning this. We define our free economy by the way it actually operates. (You are what you do.) Then we set about getting human beings to do what is necessary to improve the economy. To this one end the whole system of laws, tax incentives, creditors, social pressures, job opportunities is brought to bear. These decide where the citizen will live, what he will eat, wear, and drive, and how much time he will spend with his family. The result is a hundred million willing slaves of the economic power structure.

The Morality of Pacification

Does this sound excessive or even paranoid? If so, says Marcuse, you've been successfully pacified. You've been led to assume that what's good for the economy is good for you. The main decisions of your life revolve around the answer to this question: What do I have to do to earn a living, put food on the table and clothes on my children's backs? You've been so pacified into accepting things the way they are that you would never dream of asking the critical, the ideal question: What would I like to do with my life, and how would I like to spend all of my time? Unreal, you say? Yes. According to operational thinking it is unreal. This kind of thinking uncritically accepts the *status quo*, rules out alternatives, and eliminates ideals. Why is it that we would never dream of asking that basic human question: What would I like to do with my life?—instead of the enslaving question: What does economic necessity dictate that I do with my life?

What has happened in America, says Marcuse, is that "technological rationality" has taken over our lives. In theory, technology is neutral. This is not so in America. Our whole society is organized around the rationale of technology. Technological rationality is what guides political decisions. In other words, political decisions are based on what will foster economic productivity. Alternative goals are not merely ruled out. They aren't even considered. "Technological rationality has become political rationality," is the way Marcuse puts it. What's more, individual citizens are induced to swallow this whole process as only reasonable. In other words, technological rationality in the end becomes individual rationality. The logic of production becomes the logic of human thinking in our society. Dollars and cents thinking takes first place. All other considerations are subordinate. Money outranks sex and health as our central concern. Confer with that barometer of American preoccupations—the index of articles printed in the *Reader's Digest*.

Mind you, it's our very logic that is now governed by technology. If you presume to follow other rules of thinking, you're illogical, you're crazy. Suppose, for example, you tried to start a political party devoted to lowering production and productivity or to stopping progress. Suppose you quit work, claiming that freedom does not consist of having money or happiness in an abundance of goods. You'd be considered a subversive good-for-nothing dreamer. We cannot imagine economic freedom outside the wage-price spiral rat race, political freedom outside the established paths of American democracy, or intellectual freedom apart from the cacophonous din of the media and the "free" press. Technological rationality has become the only rationality. Bluntly, man exists for the machine, not the machine for man.

If you don't believe that you are dominated by technological rationality, consider what a truly human freedom would look like. Here it is. Does it sound "crazy"? Consider a world in which you are free from the economy, free from the necessity of making a living. It would be a world, not of idleness, but of activity. However, it would be activity performed in freedom and leisure, more play than work. No more daily struggle for existence. Such would be economic freedom.

Political freedom would be freedom from the politics and politicians that control me instead of my controlling them. It would be a world in which politicians followed Aristotle's dictum: "Friends and truth are dear, but piety requires us to honor truth above our friends." No more voting booths offering indistinguishable candidates vying for the chance to dominate and gouge you.

Finally, consider a world of intellectual freedom in which individual thought would be liberated. No longer manipulated by indoctrination, mass communication, and public opinion, the individual would be restored, and his unique creativity honored.

"A world in which I need not work for a living, in which I control my government, and in which I think my own creative thoughts. It's unreal," you say; "it's utopian." How sad that a world in which I am not chained to an economic machine, or victimized by a tyrannical politics, or controlled by the mass media seems so unreal. What could be more natural than to imagine that a man during his short space on earth could exercise his powers with dignity, master of his own fate and his own thoughts? The problem is not that this ideal is utopian. The problem rather bears witness to the power of those forces which separate us from our freedom to be who we really are.

Granted, Marcuse's diagnosis of capitalistic unfreedom goes against the grain of established American thinking. Economic slavery? We have the best standard of living in the world, don't we? Political tyranny? Where else are elections more free? Controlled thinking? Our freedom of speech is notorious around the world to the point of scandal. True, responds Marcuse. We can raise the standard—of *administered* living. We live well, provided that we remain cogs in the technological machine, serving rather than served by the laws of productivity. We are well-fed slaves, preferring this security to freedom because we see no way to becoming well fed and also free. We don't even dream of an alternative. We are likewise inextricably caught in the web of established politics and established thinking, never dreaming that there might be a way out. The political trap and the free-speech trap are closely connected. In both areas we practice a tolerance that isn't tolerance at all, but oppression. By giving every political viewpoint, every voice and every opinion a hearing, we emasculate them, good and bad alike, and cause them to be not worth hearing.

A glance at your corner drugstore's paperback book rack illustrates Marcuse's point. The pornographer shares space with Plato, as does the racist with the humanitarian. Bright packaging, not nutrition, sells cereal at the supermarket. So it is with our highly touted "marketplace of ideas." Every discussion panel has its token radical, every school committee its token student, every governing board its token black or female. Thus the opposition is institutionalized and thereby welcomed into the establishment. The man of experience and the silly exhibitionist, the truth-teller and the liar receive an equally respectful hearing. Thus, truth and criticism are trivialized and incorporated into the established order of things. All voices become merely different accents in one cultural milieu. Truly radical criticism is impossible. It used to be possible for a few people to live outside the established order of things and thereby challenge it; the adulteress, the rebel poet, the great criminal and the revolutionary did not walk the normal path. However, today we have not the adulteress, but the neurotic housewife, not the rebel poet but the hippie, not the great criminal outcast but the gangster, not the revolutionary, but the protester. The opposition has been enlisted to affirm rather than negate the established order.

In summary, it is Marcuse's claim that technological rationality has put us in a moral prison. Our politics and our very thinking are subject to its laws. Our so-called intellectual, economic and political freedoms are conditioned by this slavery. Opposition and freedom alike are part of life within the prison. It is impossible to assault the prison walls from the outside.

IMPRISONED BY YOUR OWN PROPAGANDA: DOUGLAS

Your moral beliefs are the result of the company you keep. Unbeknownst to yourself, your neighbor's propaganda puts you in a moral prison. So we were informed by the sociologist in the first part of this chapter. Next, the Marxist critique by Marcuse showed how we are made content with our prison existence. Duped by capitalism's economic propaganda, we imagine that we are free, that we are not in prison at all. We happily allow our whole lives to be controlled by the demands of technology, and wouldn't have it any other way. Let's consider now how the anthropologist claims to confirm these depressing findings. Mary Douglas in her book, *Natural Symbols*, shows how the shape of a man's morality can be predicted from the structure of the society in which he lives.[4] In other words, says the social anthropologist, tell me what a man's family and social milieu are like, and I'll give you a list of his cardinal virtues and capital sins.

Social Anthropology

Her anthropological studies have led Douglas to distinguish four types of societies, ranging from those that are highly organized and demand intense loyalty, to those that are vague, amorphous and unstructured. Structure depends on two factors: (1) the group factor: How well defined and organized is the group? (2) the individual factor, or let's call it the I-factor for short: What am I expected to do? How well defined are the demands made of the individuals? I will hold certain moral truths to be self-evident, depending upon the group factor and the I-factor of the society in which I move. In other words, though I don't realize it at all, my values depend on my society's structure. As a result, I defend these values as the most reasonable and urge them on everyone else. Were the social structure of my life to change, however, this firmly held value system would collapse like a house of cards. Then I would realize that I had been taken in by my own propaganda. Let's look at the four types of societies and the moralities to which they give rise.

First, there are societies where the group is everything, and the individual is nothing without the group. The total stress is on loyalty and on the importance of belonging. The one important thing is to know who is in and who is out. And to be put out is a fate worse than death. The group's laws are absolute. In the Greek city-state for example, civil disobedience was unthinkable, and exile was worse than capital punishment. The exile belonged to the realm of the living dead. Without a society to call his own, his individual existence had no meaning anymore. Where the group-factor totally overshadows the I-factor, the law is absolute, and ostracism is the ultimate moral sanction.

Likewise in the medieval Roman Church, excommunication was the direst of penalties; the excommunicate belonged no longer to the society of heaven or that of earth. The same utter domination of group over individual is manifest in village life of seventeenth century England as well as in the military regime of modern day West Point. Breakers of the code were "sent to Coventry" or "given the silent treatment." In a word, they were destroyed as individuals.

What moral code regulates such a social structure? It's not hard to guess. Where the group is all that matters, passive conformity is the cardinal virtue. Even if the Church were to teach that white is black and black is white, that would settle the question. Blind faith is worthy of the highest merit. So, too, the soldier. His is not to understand but to obey. Disobedience and disloyalty are the capital sins. These moral facts are beyond argument. They form the self-evident, taken for granted moral world of persons caught up in a group factor society. People without faith, people who obey no law but their own are automatically cast into the ranks of the damned.

But these "damned" become the "saved" in the second type of social structure. These are the societies where emphasis is switched from the group to the individual. Belonging to a particular group is not important. Knowing who is in and who is out is not important. Here the I-factor comes to center stage. What counts are the expectations and roles demanded of the individual. The post-technological society of the modern Western world is the primary example of an I-factor society. Tight, loyal affiliation to groups is minimal. Except for the parents-children unit, family ties are loose. Church affiliations are more fluid. Mixed marriages and cross-denominational worship become as much the rule as the exception. There is little strong loyalty to the company for which one works. Job mobility becomes the standard practice and ideal. One "hangs loose" with regard to groups. But the whole purpose is that he may develop himself and advance as an individual.

Though the group demands are few in an I-factor society, many and varied are the burdens placed upon the individual. He is expected, for example, to complete long years of education, to get a good job, and to move up the ladder continually. He is expected to acquire a car, a color TV, and an endlessly expanding list of consumer goods from electric carving knives to hygiene deodorants. His is the burden to provide all of these and more for his wife and his children.

Once again, it is not hard to guess the shape of the moral code that regulates such a society. Hard work and individual achievement are the cardinal virtues of the I-factor societies. External success is the sign of confirmation in grace for the practice of these virtues. Initiative rather than obedience, creativity rather than conformity, are praised. Withdrawal from the quest for progress, failure to use one's talents for one's own advancement and for the good of one's loved ones and of mankind—these are the capital sins in an I-factor society. The man who cares not to work or has no will to better himself will find himself condemned. Where the work-ethic is worshiped, welfare recipients become "bums," and mystics become weirdos. Again, such moral facts are considered beyond argument. They form the self-evident, taken for granted moral world of persons caught up in an I-factor society.

Third, there are societies which stress both the group-factor and the I-factor alike. And these societies, too, will have a morality all of their own. On the one hand, the group is important. Belonging is essential. Everyone knows and cares who is in and who is out. On the other hand, the roles and expectations of the individual are also highly organized and structured. I think of a society like Vatican City. The group is Roman Catholic, and it is important to belong. Individuals within the group have carefully defined roles. Each caste—pope, cardinal, bishop, priest, layman—has its privileges and duties. And within each caste, the hierarchical pecking order is understood by all. Armies, prisons, monasteries, and mental hospitals manifest a similar social structure. In this third type of society, group definition and individual role assignment both combine to tightly control the behavior of the members.

As you would imagine, disloyalty and dereliction of duty are the capital sins in a society where both group and individual are highly defined. One may fail the organization through personal weakness, but one may never question the structure itself. The cardinal virtues are those of the company man, loyalty and the efficient performance of duty. Individual initiative and critical outspokenness are not rewarded.

As a fourth example of how social structure determines morality, the anthropologist cites the society where both structure and controls are at a minimum. First, from the side of the group, "belonging" is not important. No one cares who is in or who is out. There are no formal requirements for membership. Second, there are little or no expectations placed upon the individual. He is free to develop, evolve, and act in any way he wishes, to find and to do "his own thing." Here we have the anchorites and hermits sequestered in the desert in the early Christian Church. Here, too, we put the open-house communes and pads where hippies float in and out, and the pygmy tribes that wander loosely through the African forests.

Here, the morality reflects the society's open character. The cardinal virtues are sincerity, authenticity, and fidelity to oneself. Capital sins are those against the self: hypocrisy, cruelty, and submitting to frustration. The individual escapes from the toils of social control to find his own authentic rhythms. Morality fosters this individual quest. Other people are suffused in a benign, ineffectual good will.

From examining these different types of groups, the anthropologist concludes that the morality to which you give such fervent personal allegiance is the inevitable product of the social structure in which you happen to be involved. Most of us remain unaware of this. Filled with the sense of having discovered the one true moral path, we urge others to see the light and look down upon them when they don't. We are taken in by our own propaganda. Consider, for example, the hippie pacifist of that totally unstructured type of society discussed above. Uninvolved in the regularly workaday world and detached from politics, his vague, generalized "love for all mankind" need not meet the harsh tests of real conflict. However, unaware that his easy ability to love flows from his unstructured, uninvolved social life, he wonders why politicians and generals don't love their enemies as he does, and he condemns as immoral all their warlike works and pomps.

Or consider the educated liberal clergyman caught up in the I-factor attitudes of secularized post-industrial society. He is ecumenical, social-service oriented and self-reliant. These are the cardinal virtues expected of the individual in the I-factor society in which he moves. Such a clergyman, unaware of the socially conditioned origin of his open-minded and self-reliant attitudes, adopts a morally superior attitude toward his flock. He laments their preoccupation with duty over social good works, and their unecumenical concern with orthodoxy over interchurch cooperation. Little does he realize how ill-suited his moral pronouncements are to the tightknit group-factor, I-factor structure in which his parishioners move. And the parishioners in their turn, preoccupied with loyalty and duty, look down with morally superior glances at outsiders who live in heresy and follow not the straight and narrow.

And so goes the human moral comedy. Each group holds as Gospel truth the morality which is particularly attuned to its own brand of social survival. Words like "duty" and "heresy" are rallying cries in one camp and anathema in another. Here "love" is worshiped as supreme strength; there it is denigrated as weakness; to some morality is a call to freedom, whereas for others, obedience signals the truly virtuous man. It is not the differences that surprise or dismay. It is the blissfully ignorant assumption that my differences are better than your differences. Taken in by my own propaganda, I act as if my moral principles enjoy a timeless, universal validity, whereas all other moralities are conditioned, distorted and somehow at least a little perverse.

Conclusion

"Morality as Prison" has been the theme of this chapter. In other words, there's a way that morality puts us into a box. The problem is not that our actions are controlled by morality. Autonomous self-control is the ideal of the moral adult, as we saw in the last chapter. Nor is the problem that our actions are somehow determined by others. Even the most individualistic philosophies have to come to terms with man as a *social* animal. No, morality puts us in prison to the extent that we are *unaware* of our jailers. Here, I suggest, is the escape hatch, the way out of the moral prison.

The moral jailer can be our neighbor, as we saw in section one. Every moral *Weltanschauung* is a conspiracy, the sociologist tells me. Less elegantly: "I choose my beliefs by choosing my playmates." I take on the moral values of the company I keep. The missionary tends to "go native," and the native transferred to "civilized" society tends to abandon his former "superstitions." This remains a trap and a prison so long as I don't realize what's going on. A visitor from Mars would suffer culture shock in the moral world which I take so much for granted. Can I experience this shock of recognition by seeing my own values through Martian eyes?

The moral jailer can be the technological rationality of the American economy as we saw in section two. Outrageous as it may appear, we have consented to be the servants of technology, rather than insisting that the technology serve us. Such is the burden of Marcuse's Marxist critique of American values. I can't imagine a world in which I would be free from the necessity of "working for a living." I must submit to the laws of maximum production and consumption as the price of human living. I can't think any other way. It's only logical, i.e., *techno*-logical. Deviants who would challenge this are emasculated by receiving a tolerant hearing. Incorporated into the system as the friendly opposition they are pacified and thereby rendered ineffective. It would take a rare and truly free man to break out of this economic logic to imagine for himself the possibility of a moral life centered around human values rather than production values.

In each case, the moral jailer ultimately is oneself. Imprisoned by the unconsciously arrogant walls erected by my own thought processes, I tend to assume a morally superior stance toward all those whose values differ from my own. As the anthropologist points out in section three, the shape of my morality is only a reflection of the shape of my society. However, unaware of how conditioned and rela-

tive my moral thinking is, I would have everyone follow suit. If I succeed, the damage can be irreparable. Witness the burning of here-
tics, the imprisoning of pacifists, and the conservative religious
believers whose moral lives have been shattered under the misguided
leadership of their liberal-minded pastors.

True, this chapter has painted a gloomy picture. However, this
need not be the last word. Sociologist Peter Berger has suggested that
the moral prison walls are made of cardboard, not concrete. A prison
break is possible. The cardboard walls are props. Morality is enacted
upon a stage. The proper locale of the moral life need not be prison at
all. Such is the hopeful theme of the next chapter, "Morality as
Theatre."

FOUR: MORALITY AS THEATRE

There must have been a moment, at the beginning, where we could have said—no. But somehow we missed it.

Tom Stoppard[1]

A man has as many different social selves as there are distinct groups of persons about whose opinion he cares.

William James[2]

Man being condemned to be free carries the weight of the whole world on his shoulders; he is responsible for the world and for himself as a way of being.

Jean-Paul Sartre[3]

The move from the metaphor of prison to the metaphor of theatre is a radical shift in our way of looking at moral demands. No longer are they a jailer's rules. Put yourself now on stage. Consider the program of your moral life as a script, a script that you are free to write for yourself. As William James points out in the quotation above, we wear many masks as we walk through life. We are not one self, but several. We will explore in section one the idea that morality is not so much a question of old-fashioned character. Rather, it is a matter of taking on "characters" as in a play.

This theme of freedom continues in section two. In the line from the Broadway play quoted at the head of the chapter: "There must have been a moment, at the beginning, where we could have said— no." As we will see, psychologist Allen Wheelis points to an exit out of the box of moral determinism. "You are what you do," he tells us. But here is our hope: "You can do what you choose."[4]

Finally, in section three we will listen to that philosopher of human freedom par excellence, Jean-Paul Sartre. Determinism is not the problem. Freedom is. However hard we try, we can't really succeed in giving up our freedom. "We are condemned to be free." Our attempt to evade this truth is the one capital sin. Let's enter now into the moral theatre.

MORAL CHARACTER OR CAST OF CHARACTERS?

A theatre is a freer and friendlier place than a prison. In this optimistic view of the moral life, we are all on stage. Our scripts can be filled with fun and happiness. And conversely, many and bitter are the tragedies that are acted out on stage. But the beauty of producing a stage tragedy is that I can change the script if I don't like it. I can close down the show. I can walk off the stage. I can choose to play another part or produce an entirely new show.

Prison morality sees life as serious and unchangeable. The tragedies are the tragedies of "real life." The rules are harsh, and there is no escape. Theatre morality rests on the great revelation that "real life" is played out on a world stage. As Shakespeare said in *King Lear*: "When we are born, we cry that we are come to this great stage of fools." Or, in contemporary lyrics: "Life is a cabaret, old chum!" I can play the fool or the wise man. I can dance in the cabaret or don the costume of the tragic victim. In the moral prison, the focus was on the oppressive determinisms of society and the economy. In the moral theatre, however, the focus is on me, the player, the chooser of roles, the writer of scripts, and the producer of my life drama. Hope and freedom replace despair and determinism.

The implications for moral responsibility of this reversal of viewpoint are shattering. Take, for example, the person who is addicted to America's favorite drug, alcohol. If he wants to be free of this addiction, it makes all the difference in the world whether he sees himself in a moral prison or as an actor on a moral stage. In his prisoner self-image, he is the victim of physiological dependency, social pressures, and unconscious psychological forces. His imagination is trapped in the prison. He sees no escape. He'll spend years in therapy, uncovering insights into his prisoner existence. However, the addiction goes on. He'll never walk as a free man outside the prison walls.

The maverick psychiatrist Thomas Szasz gives an entirely different reading of the so-called addict's moral situation. Where Alcoholics Anonymous considers alcoholism to be an incurable disease, Szasz sees it as a script.[5] This dramatic production called "alcoholism" bills the "patient-victim" as the star. As his chosen life-drama, his role has great internal significance, and he plays his part with gusto. Nevertheless, since the so-called "addiction" is based upon a reversible life decision, the potential for "cure," i.e., a change of script, is present. There is basis for hope.

Following the leads of Szasz and Berne, "Lush" is one of the alcoholic games analyzed by Claude Steiner.[6] Lush was taught early in life that "children should be seen and not heard." "Don't think!" "Don't make your own decisions." While fidelity to this script brought parental approval when he was young, it is totally inappropriate in the adult world. Now he is a non-entity, ignored, starved for attention and sexually deprived. Lush's alcoholic script is his way of adapting to the adult world his outmoded "Don't think!" childhood game. Since he feels that he is not allowed to get attention and satisfaction from others on the basis of his own positive decisions, he gets them the hard way through his self-destructive drinking. Better *negative* attention than no attention at all. Lush becomes the problem child to be persecuted or rescued or humored. Also, his drugged condition brings two excellent side benefits. First, with his inhibitions temporarily lifted, he is free to go on the prowl for the sexual satisfaction that he so sorely misses. Second, his mind is fogged out. He is in no danger of violating the parental taboo against thinking for himself or making adult decisions. So for Lush, the payoffs of the script are big. But the stakes are high. Lush's psychological gains are achieved at the cost of a hard game played with his own bodily tissue.

Closing down this hit show called "Lush" is difficult but not impossible. What he needs is a new dramatic production where the star can get the attention and sexual satisfaction that he craves without paying the high price exacted by the script of "Lush." To accomplish this, he'll need to feel that as an adult he does indeed have permission to think clearly and make his own decisions and hence, paradoxically, that he does have permission *not* to drink, *not* to fog out his mind. Then he'll be able to learn to get positive recognition and attention to replace the negative variety with which he had to rest content before. In order (probably best with skillful therapy) to learn his new role effectively, he'll have to lay off the drug for a year or more. But if he succeeds in changing the script, the drug will be no longer a problem. The new drama will achieve the same gains and better than the game of "Lush" and at far less cost.

This dramatic theory of human behavior has been used mainly to illuminate deviant games such as "Lush." However, the point of the theatre view of the morals game here is that all human action and therefore all moral behavior is susceptible to such analysis. In a word, morality is a learned script. Often the actors go so far as to explicitly set a stage and dress up in the appointed costumes. And on this stage, as in the legitimate theatre, truly marvelous things occur. Take the obvious example of a wedding. Look at the clergyman, the bride and groom, the attendant men and ladies, and the bride's paterfamilias all dolled up for the 5 o'clock ceremony. As the musicians play the score, the actors do their minuet down the aisle. The clergyman waves his arms. Bride and groom are transformed into husband and wife. What at 4:45 p.m. would have been morally condemned as fornication is at 5:15 p.m. blessed and smiled on by all.

Similarly, the judge dons his robes to condemn a man to death. Offstage, in the street, this act would be the crime of conspiracy to murder. In the courthouse, done in proper costume, it becomes the virtuous execution of duty, much as the soldier's uniform transforms husband and father into paid killer. Travel from culture to culture, and you will see the stage magic enacted everywhere, albeit with different scripts, costumes and denouements.

And in a less dramatic way we put on various faces and different roles as we walk onto different social scenes. I become the thoughtful son, the pillar of the community, the efficient businessman, the lusty realist as I move in turn from home to church to office to Friday night poker with the boys. The "Thou shalt nots" of the family dinner table are freely violated at a convention of Elks, and costumes that would be sinful in church and scandalous downtown bring admiration and applause at the beach.

The point of this theatrical view of morality is simply this. Looked at from this angle, moral rules and obligations are not oppressive impositions by social and economic forces beyond my control. Quite the opposite. They are fragile scripts whose successful enactment requires the cooperation of me the moral actor. If I choose not to play, these seemingly solid prison walls collapse. They are revealed for what they are—cardboard walls on an empty moral stage.

To call moral rules a script is not to say that the script can be easily changed. There are fellow actors on my various stages who don't want *their* scripts endangered by *my* miscues. When I try to close up a show—be it by a divorce to end a marriage or by changing from a meat-eater to a vegetarian diet—I'll not lack obstacles to overcome any more than does the alcoholic who changes from unthinking Lush to responsible decision-maker. Getting a new show on the road is hard work too. I need a new stage, new props and fellow-players, and I must struggle to learn the lines. The point is, that in spite of these difficulties, there is hope. Other scripts than my current ones are possible. I see other people playing them all the time. I am not hopelessly immured in a moral prison.

Is this theatrical view a prescription for moral anarchy? Do I have any obligation to mold a consistent character, to integrate my life into a totality? Is it up to me to follow the imperative that Polonius addressed to Laertes in Shakespeare's *Hamlet*: "To thine own self be true, and it must follow, as the night the day, thou canst not then be false to any man"? Indeed, am I one self, or many selves? Does the truly good man in the course of his life through his moral decisions hammer out a consistent character? Or may he be content to move on and off many stages in many different characters?[7]

Clearly, these questions are fundamental. The answers I give to them will reflect the philosophy of man that underlies my life and moral thinking. Answers now are premature. In later chapters we will explore some of the major philosophical alternatives. To cite just one example, the answer you give to the above questions will depend to a great extent upon just how rational your philosophy is. Scientific and rational thinkers have little toleration for inconsistency. Contradictions must be reconciled. The whole picture must be self-consistent and must make sense. Morality will reflect this. Its goal will be to form a coherent self, a consistent character. A philosophy, on the other hand, which has more space for the pluralistic and irrational, will be less concerned with moral consistency.

Is It Normal To Wear Many Masks?

Premature consistency can become rigidity. A "firm moral character" might be more a signal of inflexibility than of strength. There is a widely held psychological and moral assumption that everyone should develop a firm sense of self-identity. The person who experiences many selves within him is thereby induced to feel guilty, unhealthy, and even immoral. But what if it is normal to wear many masks, to play many roles? And so what if they are inconsistent? We do not demand that an actor playing in three shows should make his three scripts consistent with each other. I play out my moral life on many stages in different social scenes. My self is many-sided. Or better, I have many selves. In this view, to suppress or deny one or other self is a form of suicide. I am killing off my possibilities, my potential selves. It is in my power to define myself as warm or cold, sexy or plain, confident or inferior, disciplined or self-indulgent. Ignoring this fact, the rigidly consistent person can torture himself with questions such as: "Why am I X when I really should be Y?" He should admit instead: "I am X and Y—what do I want to do about it?"

Society's excessive concern for moral consistency makes for needless worry about script and game discrepancies. The heterosexual worries about occasional homosexual leanings. Husband and wife worry about fantasies of infidelity, the businessman about a weekend drunken spree. The ascetic is disgusted with his own materialism. A woman who sees herself as lively and active goes up the wall during moments of quiet. A man who prides himself on his strength is pained at moments of weakness. And if in my mind's eye I am a submissive follower, I panic when thrust into a leadership role. Why need I be so one-dimensional? Why can't I allow many possibilities to find expression in many selves and many roles? It may well be that some of my scripts are so disruptive and make me so unhappy that I should try to change them. However, for morality as theatre, diversity of scripts need not in itself be a source of guilt and disgust. Such diversity may merely signal my rich variety of interests, potentials and selves.

The trick is to express this richness and flexibility without chaos. There are strong pressures toward consistency. Spouses depend on each other to keep the family and the household going. They need to divide responsibilities. Each expects the other to do his share, i.e., to play a predictable role. We find it hard to tolerate inconsistencies even in those on whom we are not dependent. The wildly unpredictable person is branded "unreliable" and punished by being left alone. Predictable behavior we reward. "I can count on you" we say. And, of course, the more you can be counted on to react in a standardized way, the more constricted is your identity, and fewer are the scripts you play.

Pressures such as these tend to put us back in the moral prison. The theatre view of morality loosens up these bonds. Many scripts need not signify an unreliable person or a wishy-washy Charlie Brown. They can be an affirmation of rich potential. In the words of Walt Whitman: "Do I contradict myself? Very well then, I contradict myself. (I am large. I contain multitudes.)"

If I don't like the roles I am playing now, I am indeed free to change. Consider now the program of moral freedom that is spelled out by Allen Wheelis.

YOUR AUTOBIOGRAPHY IS A STORY OF CHOICES, NOT CAUSES: WHEELIS

Freedom is no mere concept dwelling in a philosopher's heaven. Freedom is not to be found in the insights that bubble and babble forth from the psychiatrist's couch. Freedom is not contained in a pill or dispensed by a drug. No doctor or therapist, no god or guru can make me free. Freedom is nowhere to be found outside of myself. Freedom is not mysterious, elusive or invisible. The locus of freedom is in human action. Freedom dwells in the highly visible, concrete, tangible world of human action—not just anybody's human action but *my* human action. Our freedom and our hope, according to Wheelis, rest on two strong pillars: (1) We are what we do; and (2) We can do what we choose. Let's examine each in turn.

We Are What We Do

In the common idiom, "actions speak louder than words." If a man fancies himself to be a great reader and scholar, I might take him at his word. However, my opinion of him will change if I find out from his intimates that for every five minutes of reading he spends five hours in front of the TV. His scholarly pretensions notwithstanding, I'll put him down as an afficionado of the boob tube rather than of the library.

Our would-be scholar, however, does not lose his reputation by spending a single New Year's weekend in an orgy of televised football. A single shop-lifted candy bar does not make an honest woman into a thief. A single "gay" encounter does not transform the happily married man into a homosexual. Nor does overindulgence at one cocktail party signal alcoholism. It is repeated action, integrated into my whole life pattern, that transforms me. But such repeated and patterned action does indeed shape my identity. I literally become what I do.

An alcoholic is not someone who takes a drink; rather he is a person who builds his whole life around alcohol, whether as an overt alcoholic who indulges or a dry alcoholic who faithfully attends AA and helps rescue those who are still wet. You don't become an automobile driver the day you pass the driving test. You become a driver when your whole life centers around your car, when you feel crippled and marooned without it, when happiness is a well automobile. Similarly, the candy-bar shoplifter really becomes a thief when, encouraged by her "success," she begins to plan her forays, to take a keen delight in anticipating and reminiscing about them, to lift more and more expensive items, and to base her personal budget on the money she gets from selling them.

In a word, according to Wheelis, it is actions and not good intentions that make me into the person I am. If I have any doubt about this, all I need to consider is how difficult it is to break out of such integrated patterns of activity. This grip that action has on my personal identity can be a shocking revelation. The shoplifter may try to give up her habit, the alcoholic his drink, or the driver his car. And a great vacuum descends upon their lives. They stumble around wondering how they can possibly live through the day. It's impossible for the shoplifter to imagine a life in which she would never take anything from a store again. The prospect of life without another drink sends the alcoholic into depression and despair. And the driving addict who tried to give up his automobile, concludes that this was a futile gesture. "It's impossible to be without a car," he tells himself. "It is an extension of my legs. I'm not free; I cannot lead a human life without it."

We Can Do What We Choose

The car freak realizes: "I am a driver; the automobile has really become a part of who I am." The drunk wakes up and realizes: "My God, I *am* an alcoholic; drinking is my life, is me." And the shoplifter faces herself: "I have become a thief; I *am* a thief; I can't imagine life without it." No claims, no mere good will, no pretensions can obscure the devastating clarity with which our actions point to who we are. So compelling and so unmistakable is this acid test of action, that I may acquiesce in despair at the verdict. I am a thief. I am an alcoholic. I am a TV addict or a car freak or a homosexual. So be it. That's my nature. It was written in the stars.

To leap to such pessimistic conclusions misses the point. What action has done, action can undo. It was not fate or the gods that made me who I am today. It was the actions flowing from my past choices. They have given me the identity which I now possess, an identity which is indeed hard to change—but not impossible. If I change my overall pattern of choice and action, I can change my very identity which now seems so firm and overpowering. Wheelis' thrust toward freedom is two-pronged. Not only is it the case that "we are what we do," but it is likewise true that "we can do what we choose."

It may be a fact that I am a thief or a gourmand, a husband or a rabbi. For such have my past actions made me. But this *fact* need not be my *destiny*, says Wheelis. I need not pronounce a final "so be it," a solemn "Amen" over this fact. I need not give up and resign myself to being "just the way I am." Right now, to be sure, I am just the way I am. But people can change. They do. Crooks reform their lives, and honest men become thieves. To cover up this fact is to abjure responsibility for my life and identity. I shift the center of gravity from powers within myself that are subject to my control to vague and uncontrollable outside forces which, with my consent, make me their victim.

"We can do what we choose." This promises, however, no facile and quick change of identity like an actor putting on a new mask or costume. It takes months and years of practice and rehearsal to get into a new role. We are not machines in which defective and undesirable parts can be replaced without disturbing the rest of the machine We are integrated organisms. A change in the part means a change in the whole organism. This is at once our weakness and our strength.

It is a weakness in that it makes change difficult. When one part of my life goes, whether it is alcohol or a wife, homosexual encounters or honest business dealings, the shock reaches to every part of my identity. In every dimension of my life I must painfully shape with my actions and integrate a whole new person. This is similar to when husband and wife become mother and father upon the arrival of their firstborn. The baby is not just one more mouth to feed. Far from it. The little one's arrival disrupts the whole organic family unit. The entrance upon the scene of this seven pounds of human flesh leaves no dimension of the family unscathed. Patterns of sleeping, eating, working, recreating, and lovemaking must be restructured and reintegrated before husband and wife achieve their harmonious new identities as father and mother. These adjustments are often slow and painful. But they are profound. And this is the strength that is proper to organic change.

Change a small part of a machine, and the rest of the machine remains unaffected. However, change a small but significant pattern of action in a person's life, and you challenge his whole identity. Organic changes are painful and slow. This is their weakness. However, small changes effect great and profound results. This is their strength. Change an action repeatedly and consistently, and there is no part of your identity that will remain unaffected. "We are what we do."

"And we can do what we choose"—*provided that* we are aware of alternatives. To the extent that I am blind to these I keep myself locked in the moral prison. I see no way out. I don't live my life, but my life lives me. Wheelis gives the marvelous example of an ant scurrying around on the pavement of a supermarket parking lot and getting crushed under the wheel of a departing car. There was an alternative for the ant.[8] It could have lodged itself on a wheel of a car and been thereby whisked away to an ant's paradise, a picnic in the park. But the ant, aware of no such alternatives, was crushed to death by forces beyond its control.

There are indeed some things that are beyond my control, such as the law of gravity, my physical height, and the weather outside. To such necessities there are not alternatives. But I live under another kind of necessity and it is quite arbitrary. It comes from blaming forces outside of myself for what could be under my own control. "I'd like to marry you," a man tells his secretary, "but I can't, because I'm already married." (There is an alternative: divorce and remarriage.) "I'd like to live sober," says the problem drinker, "but I can't help drinking." (There is an alternative: don't drink.) "I'd like to live in a warmer climate, but my job keeps me stuck in this wintery wasteland." (There is an alterative: quit your job, and look for work in sunnier climes.) So the wife, the booze, and the job all get blamed for ruining my life. In thus shifting control from myself to forces outside of myself, I become blind to the alternatives that I really do have. I come to believe sincerely that I have no choice but to live in this self-made prison. I am my own jailer, but I'll never set myself free, because I pretend that there are others who have the key—not myself. "We can do what we choose," says Wheelis. However, absolutely essential to this freedom is a clear-sighted recognition of the possibilities that are open to me.

Isn't it the case that the problem drinker *is* addicted? And can't I say, when I look back at all the circumstances, that my particular marriage was in the cards for me, and the arrival of each succeeding child only serves to tighten more closely this marital bond (or noose!)? And isn't it true that money doesn't grow on trees? The economy exercises a ruthless control over me, and so I have no choice but to submit to the necessities of my job. In other words, am I really so far from wrong when I blame my helplessness on the wife, the booze, and the job? Doctors study alcoholics; sociologists study marriages; economists study industry. And all come up with reasons, laws and *causes* which *determine* the behavior of their subjects. And leaving science aside, can't I come up with an explanation for everything that has ever happened to me? Even the coincidences in my life can be explained when I examine the chain of events that led up to them.

I can write my autobiography from two differing points of view, one in terms of *causes*, and the other in terms of *choices*. Let's look in turn at each of these ways of creating my life's story. The word "creating" is used advisedly. The book of my life is not sitting passively on the shelf waiting to be *read*. That was the prison view of morality. In the theatre view, it is a story which I creatively write in radically different ways.

In the scientific story of man, there is a reason for everything. And if I knew all the forces and influences on a man's behavior, I could unerringly predict exactly how he would act. My so-called choices are a product of all the outer causes that give them shape. I necessarily choose what will bring me satisfaction and reward in preference to unsatisfactory and less rewarding ways of action. Psychologist B.F. Skinner gives a contemporary expression to this deterministic model of man. The question, he tells us, is not whether human action is free or conditioned. Man necessarily acts in the way that is most rewarding to him. The only question is one of control. We can allow others to seek their rewards in a haphazard fashion. Or we can control their behavior by controlling the rewards.

Rewards. It was the thought of a hot shower and a hot cup of coffee that got me out of bed this morning. My heavy limbs and fogged-out mind conspired to keep me under the covers. But the price would be too high: a skipped breakfast and co-workers wondering about my late arrival to the office. On arriving at work, I sit down at the typewriter to compose these pages. My mind is blank. Nothing comes. I reach for a nearby philosophy book. The reading is tough, but not so tough as staring at a blank page waiting to be filled. The phone rings. Relief! I prolong the conversation. This is a better distraction than the philosophy book. Conversation ends. I face the typewriter again. My writing has a deadline to meet, and the thought of missing it gets me started. In the long run, this pressure makes hard work the more satisfying behavior. Soon it is time to appear in the classroom to give a lecture. I go, of course. There are thirty-five students expecting me. This plus the conditioning of innumerable past classroom days makes my appearance inevitable. I am driven not only toward social and psychological rewards, but toward biological ones too. My stomach signals the advent of lunch hour. I have to eat. Otherwise, I'd get a headache and would be unable to work effectively. And so it goes. Everything I do has a reason. I can go through the days and weeks of my life listing everything I do. Of each action, I inquire: What did I get out of it? The answer to this question gives me a clue to the reward, i.e., to the influences operating on every level that caused this action to take place. What I am doing is writing my life story in terms of causes. The sum of all these causes has made me into the man that I am today. Even my illusions of freedom are the product of my physical, biological, psychological and social environments. It is to these forces that I point when I'm asked who's responsible for my life. Like the ant in the parking lot, I'm aware of no real alternatives. And like the ant, one day these forces will snuff out my life and end a story over whose direction I never had any control.

But this very same life story with these very same events can be written in a radically different way. What makes the deterministic story seem so inevitable is that at each step of the way all alternatives are rigorously excluded. But the alternatives *are* there. I need not have gotten out of bed this morning. I could have snoozed an extra half hour (many people do), or arisen an hour earlier (again, many people do just that), or phoned in sick to the office and sacked out for the morning (a not exactly unheard-of alternative). What had seemed like a necessity to get up in the morning becomes my free choice to rise and shine, when I am aware of the range of options open to me.

On arriving at the office and sitting down to compose at the typewriter, my mind seemed blank. No words would come. I reached for a book, an easy distraction. There were, however, alternatives. No need to abdicate responsibility and blame forces outside my control: "I can't help myself," the writer likes to say; "I have 'writer's block.' " When I become aware of my alternatives, I see that it is I who am blocking the writer in me. What seemed like the necessity of a psychological block becomes a free choice. Besides staring at a blank page in self-induced paralysis, I have the alternative of writing something, anything. I still know the English language. I have *some* ideas related to what I want to say. What I write may not be perfect, but I can start some words flowing. I may feel paralyzed, but I'm not. The proof of the matter is to actually write a word, a phrase, a sentence. Then I see that "writer's block" is not a compulsive psychological disease, but a free decision not to write.

The phone rings. Too bad! A distraction. I have to stop what I'm doing. It's strange how few people realize that there is an alternative to the "necessity" of answering the phone, viz., let it ring! Aware of this option, I can no longer honestly complain about the tyranny of the telephone. I do have a choice. And if I answer it every time it imperiously rings, it's because I am a willing slave.

Time to appear in the classroom to teach. I must stop what I am doing and go. "Must?" On any given day I can just not show. This has been known to happen. And students have been known to relish an unexpected day off. Indeed I need never enter a classroom again. There are other jobs besides teaching. Aware of these alternatives, I see that my appearance in the classroom is an act, not of necessity, but of freedom.

Lunch time. Gotta eat. "Gotta?" Am I eating because it's lunch time or because I'm hungry? Would a brisk walk serve to refresh me as much or more than eating food that I don't really need? Or a twenty minute nap followed by a cup of coffee? I have the option, too, of working through lunch hour buoyed up by the hope of getting home an hour sooner as a result. Seen in the context of these alternatives, eating lunch as usual is clearly more a free choice than a biological necessity.

It's up to me whether I want to write my autobiography as a story of freedom or a story of necessity. The two stories are not contradictory to each other. In a way they are complementary. The decisions I have made in the past decades of my life have made me into the person I am today. They have *determined* the person I have come to *be*. "We are what we do," says Wheelis. However, my very awareness of what I have become and of the actions that have made me into what I am—this very awareness makes freedom possible. The actions of my life have alternatives. By changing the course of my actions, I can change the course of my life. I can thereby change who I am. "We may do what we choose," says Wheelis. To be sure, circumstances have their impact. If I'm born and raised in Boston, it is unlikely that I'll grow up speaking Hindi. Circumstances limit my options. However, the fact remains that I do have options. And I can choose from among the options that I have. Or I can change my circumstances and thus bring a whole new range of options into my ken. The reformed drinker can continue to go to cocktail parties and exercise his option of drinking plain ginger ale. Or he can open up for himself a new set of options by taking up social activities that don't center around drink.

So there is an interplay of determinism and freedom. Determined by my past decisions ("we are what we do"), I am nevertheless free to change ("we may do what we choose"). More than any other philosopher, the French existentialist Jean-Paul Sartre provides a philosophical underpinning for this view of the moral life as an uncompromising exercise of freedom. We are ready now to see one philosophical picture of man that is implied by this emphasis on moral freedom.

PHILOSOPHER OF RADICAL FREEDOM: SARTRE

There is no question for Sartre of proving that man is free. Rather, freedom is the central fact, the overwhelming burden, of human existence. Man is "condemned to be free." There is no way I can be rid of the burden of absolute responsibility for my life. In our brief outline of Sartre's philosophy, we will see as it were a laboratory case of how intimately an ethics is linked to one's philosophy of man.

There Is No Objective Good

For Sartre, as for Wheelis, there is a side to life in which I am the plaything of circumstances beyond my control. There is mandatory necessity, or "facticity," as Sartre calls it. I find myself thrust onto the scene of this world's stage with no questions asked. I turn up. I'm there. Why? What is the meaning of it all, the meaning of my life? There is no thing or anyone outside of myself that can answer these questions. In itself, human life is an absurdity. It begins without meaning and ends in nothingness. No one can give me a reason to be rather than not to be or to make one decision rather than another. Any meaning I have will be completely my own creation. Anything is possible.

Most of us can't face this utter absurdity and limitless freedom. We prefer to think that there is a plan for man that is written in the heavens like the blueprint for next year's automobile models. When the new cars roll off the assembly line in Detroit, they are made according to specification. Each model has its own built-in limitations and its own potentialities. Its purpose is clear. It has a particular function. And if the auto measures up to the pre-planned level of performance, it passes as a "good car." In some such way, we like to think that there is a divine blueprint for man. It's as if God designed a "human nature" with built-in specifications, clearly designated functions, and a pre-given goal. And when man comes off the divine assembly line and into this world, his path is clearly laid out for him.

The meaning of his life is clear. His purpose in life is to conform to this divine plan, to this "natural law." In metaphysical terms, we pretend that man has a ready-made essence, and that existence on this earth is simply a matter of following out this predetermined essential meaning of life.

We are afraid, says Sartre, to face the fact that man is a radically different kind of being from automobiles, stones, or cabbages. For automobiles, the plan comes first and the assembly line comes next. More technically, for automobiles, essence precedes existence. Not so, in the case of humans. Man is the only kind of being for whom existence precedes essence. I first exist. I first turn up on the scene. Only then do I create my essence, my meaning of life, the person I am going to be.

A dog is "species-specific." His doggy life is predictable. Inevitably he'll live it out with his doggy actions in a doggy world. But humans are "world-open." There is no given human world, human essence. My world is mine to make. It is not enough to say that man is free. Sartre goes further. "Man *is freedom*," he tells us. This sets human existence radically apart from everything else.

And since man is freedom, God cannot exist. Encounter with such an omnipotent, all-knowing freedom would destroy the chance of human freedom. More than that, it would destroy my very humanness. It is precisely freedom that defines me as a human being. To believe in God, then, is to commit suicide as a human being. There is a strong temptation to do this, and many yield. For if I can shift the burden of my life's meaning to a power outside of myself, I am relieved of responsibility for making my own moral decisions. In this vein, people will ask their pastors: "Tell me what to do." Or faced with a decision they will cop a religious plea: "I can't do that; my religion forbids it." And so we live in "bad faith." But more about bad faith in a minute. It's an ethical term.

Man's Choices Create Human Nature

Recall that a morally good action is one which is faithful to what it means to be a human being in all that that involves. In other words, your norm of moral good and evil depends on your philosophy of man. This philosophy expresses your convictions about what it means to be a human person. And your ethics enjoins you to act accordingly, to be faithful to your fundamental convictions. What ethical norm, then, would you expect to follow from a philosophy of man such as

Sartre's? Sartre's analysis of the human predicament has led him to conclude that man is freedom. So you are not surprised that his ethics enjoins you to be faithful to this freedom which is at the heart of the very meaning of human. In other words, any action that I freely, sincerely and authentically choose is morally good. And moral evil is the opposite of this. It lies in the act that is insincere and hypocritical; it lies in the choice that is inauthentic or capricious; most basically, moral evil consists in the attempt to evade that freedom and responsibility that defines me as a man. This, for Sartre, is the meaning of "bad faith," the original and capital sin.

There can be no greater self-betrayal than to treat myself as a thing, an object, a finished product. No matter how far along in life I have come, I can never sit back, relax, and tell myself: "That's it; this is me; I am what I am and there's nothing more to do about it." There are countless ways in which I am tempted to live in this bad faith, countless ways of treating myself as an unfree object rather than as a unique center of freedom.

It is bad faith, for example, to tie oneself to a moral code. This argues, paradoxically enough, for the immorality of all moralities which originate outside of myself. It is a betrayal of my freedom to submit my life to external moral rules. There is no pre-given external plan which I can follow with assurance. And to pretend that there is such a plan is to live a lie. My destiny as a man is to *create* the meaning of human nature, not to follow a "natural law." This is not to say that people don't commonly follow a conventional code of morality as a matter of course. They are not thereby relieved of moral responsibility. My decisions are creating the very meaning of human for me. If I look in the mirror and don't like what I see, I have no one but myself to blame. Society did not make me a conventional man. That was accomplished by my decisions to follow the ruts of conventional thinking. *Not* to decide is to decide. There is no escape from freedom. We are "condemned to be free."

If morality is totally created by myself, if there are no outside clues as to which is the good and true path to follow, are we not then in a state of moral anarchy? There can be no objectivity in morals, says Sartre. Morality rests one hundred percent in the subjectivity of the moral agent. Is this not a prescription for chaos? Every man picks and chooses his moral values as he pleases—good and evil decided by a toss of the coin. This seems not to be responsibility but the depth of moral irresponsibility. Not so, says Sartre. Moral decisions are to be made authentically. Let's see what he means.

This is not an "anything goes" morality. I must make my

choices freely and sincerely, but not capriciously. The human project which is my moral life is not a trivial undertaking. I am engaged in nothing less than the creation of human nature. Such a project has a divine sound to it. And indeed, for Sartre, man has this god-like power. So jealous is Sartre of this power that he cannot conceive of a God who would transcend man. For such a God would be an overwhelming threat to the one thing which sets human existence apart from all other existence. Man is the only being who exists for himself. He is destined to decide his own meaning, to create his own nature. Moral decisions, then, are to be made not capriciously, but authentically. By "authentic" Sartre means that in choosing for myself, I am choosing for all. For in choosing for myself, I am choosing the very meaning of human. I must choose in the way that I would want any other human being in my unique situation to choose. Of course, no one else could ever be uniquely me, in my particular unique situation. Even I myself five minutes from now will be a slightly different person in an entirely new and unique situation. That is why it is bad faith to rest on my past choices. I am never "finished." But uniqueness doesn't mean anything goes. Freedom does not mean capriciousness. When I choose in good faith I am aware that I am using my freedom to create the meaning of man. There is no objective guide or power to show me the way. All the more then must I use my utter freedom authentically and responsibly. There is no built-in divine failsafe. My decisions are mine alone, and the consequences are mine alone to live with.

Whether or not you agree with Sartre, he provides a valuable challenge. He pushes freedom and subjectivity in morals to their very limit. The norm of moral good does not rest on *what* I do. It is not at all objective. The norm of moral good rests entirely on *how* I choose. It is completely subjective. You cannot compare objective actions, one with another, and decide upon their morality. I see a bombardier raining death on the enemy and a nurse below tending the wounded. I cannot correctly label the former action evil, or the latter, good. *What* is being done tells me nothing about the moral values at stake. There is no objective moral order to guide me. It is the *how* of the free decisions that counts. A man could be a nurse on the battlefield in bad faith. Perhaps he avoids fighting on the front lines because of a secret cowardice and hides his responsibility for this even from himself behind the role of nurse. In attempting to evade his freedom, he is living in bad faith. And conversely, the bombardier could be acting in free and sincere authenticity. His actions as a warrior are done with eyes open, with consequences freely accepted, and in awareness of the image of man for which he is fighting. In a word, for Sartre, morality consists not in the objective *what*, but the subjective *how*. There is no sense or meaning in an absurd world except the sense and meaning that I freely create for myself.

SUMMARY OF MORALITY AS THEATRE

This chapter has been an essay at breaking out of the moral prison. Freedom is the key, and the key is in my pocket, mine to use whenever I choose. When I unlock the prison gates and pass through them, I find that I am walking out onto a stage. Morality is a learned script, as psychologists Berne and Szasz have pointed out. Once I see my moral life as a drama that I am acting out rather than as obedience to a set of commands issuing from a lawgiver, then I am free to consider changing the role and the script, closing down the show I don't like and setting about the production of a new one. This dramatic view opens up the possibility, too, that I can follow many scripts, play many roles. I can make room to express the many potential selves I carry within me, without suppressing this richness in the name of developing an overly rigid moral character. I can travel through life as a cast of characters.

Wheelis gives us a program for translating this freedom into concrete everyday living. First, "we are what we do," he tells us. The focus is on action. And second, "we can do what we choose." This is our hope. If we change our actions then our moral character(s) will necessarily follow suit. What action has done, action can undo. The *fact* of what I am does not have to become my *destiny*. I can change. I need not write my life's story in terms of causes. Though I was not aware of them, at every step along the way I had alternatives. My autobiography is just as truly a story of choices as a story of causes.

Existentialist philosopher Jean-Paul Sartre provides a philosophical basis for this freedom of which Wheelis speaks. Man is the only being who is world-open, who chooses his own nature. Outside of man, there is no meaning, only absurdity. There is no predetermined plan to follow. My essence is my own to choose. In a word, man is freedom. Sartre's ethics of moral freedom follows from this view of man. I am morally good when I am faithful to what I am, when I shoulder courageously the burden of creating my own nature. The attempt to evade this responsibility is moral evil or "bad faith." I deny the one thing that makes me human when I try to hide behind roles or rules or moral codes. Nothing outside of me can point to the path that I must follow. There is no objective morality. The norm of the moral life is one hundred percent subjective. My whole meaning lies in the responsible use of my own freedom.

Sartre, at least in his pre-Marxist phase, had a very atomic view of man. Each person is an island of freedom unto himself. Encounter with another person, another freedom, means conflict. One or the other of us must submit. One must lose his freedom. However we try, we can't both succeed in remaining free. What passes for love is really sadomasochism. One dominates. The other submits. Clearly this view makes for a very pessimistic social philosophy.

There is another group of philosophers who agree with Sartre that morality is an affair of the will and the heart rather than of mind and head. But for these philosophers, true freedom flowers when bathed in the grace of love. I need not walk alone in my quest to grow free. Let us look in the next chapter at what I call "Will-Power Morality," i.e., morality based on love, on feeling.

FIVE: WILL-POWER MORALITY

Real love is only possible in the freedom of society; and freedom is only possible when love is a reality.

Edward Carpenter

Le coeur a ses raisons que la raison ne connait point. (The heart has its reasons which reason does not understand.)

Blaise Pascal

The course of human history is determined, not by what happens in the skies, but by what takes place in the hearts of men.

Sir Arthur Keith

We can artificially divide mankind into two groups, the lovers and the thinkers. There are heart-people, and there are mind-people. In technical terms, the first group tends toward *emotivism* in ethics; the second is on the side of *cognitivism*. The cognitivist puts his faith in intelligence. *Know* what you choose, he says. Moral choices must above all be *reasonable*. Cognitive ethics is the subject of the next chapter. The emotivist, on the other hand, trusts his feelings. He takes for his own the motto of Pascal quoted above: "The heart has its reasons which reason does not understand." Ethics based on feeling is the subject of this chapter.

To this general camp belong two philosophical approaches which are widely influential in the English-speaking world today. The first is commonly labeled "situation ethics." For the situationist, *love* is the basis of ethics. The American moralist Joseph Fletcher has done most to popularize this position.[1] We outline it in section one: "Love Is Enough." For the emotivist, the springs of moral action flow from our *feelings*. British philosophers A.J. Ayer[2] and Charles Stevenson[3] have been prominent exponents of this position. We outline it in section two: "Feeling Is All There Is."

This chapter stresses the non-rational approaches to morality. In keeping with this theme, we conclude the chapter by showing briefly how the light of *myth* can be brought to bear upon the ethical reasons that "the heart has . . . which reason does not understand."

LOVE IS ENOUGH: FLETCHER

"Situation ethics" is the label co-opted today by this ethics based on loving concern for others. Sartrean ethics, too, deserves to be called situational. Recall the last chapter. For Sartre there are no objective clues to moral good and evil; there are no external laws. Each decision stands uniquely alone. In other words, each decision is made in a particular *situation* which never has been or ever will be reduplicated. Therefore, there can be no universal rules to guide me in the unique circumstances in which each particular moral decision occurs. In denying all place to outside law, Sartre's brand of situation ethics is antinomian (a ten-dollar word meaning "antilegalistic").

The "New Morality"

The situation ethics which we are about to consider now is not of this antinomian variety. Joseph Fletcher's ethics based on loving concern for others is indeed a "situationism." Every moral decision occurs in a unique situation and therefore cannot submit blindly to universal moral laws. Fletcher is not antinomian, however, and this for two reasons. First, Fletcher holds that moral rules derived from past experience or even from religion can be used as guidelines for my moral decisions—and this without bad faith. I am not so free that my moral life is completely up for grabs at every decisive challenge. There are clues to good and evil outside myself. I do not create good and evil completely out of my own free and sincere choices. Also, and this is the second reason why Fletcher is not antinomian, there are demands put upon my moral responsibility by the situation itself. Each situation is a law unto itself demanding my moral response. What kind of law is this that at once is *universally* demanding and yet is *unique* to each situation? It is the law of *love*.

"Love thy neighbor as thyself," says Fletcher. Taking his clue from Christianity, Fletcher extolls love as the supreme and central human and moral value. Love is the sole norm of morality. Love is a law unto itself. Any action performed out of loving concern is by that fact morally good. "Love, and do what you will," Fletcher might say paraphrasing Augustine.

But not just any old kind of love will do. Ancient Greek philosophy distinguished three kinds of love, and these hold good today. There is the love of friendship (called *philia* in Greek); there is romantic love (or *eros*); and there is love which is a universal good will —the Greeks called this *agapé*. The Greeks seem to have been more sensitive to the different kinds of loving; their language reflects this. For all our obsession with love in both psychology and song we have no English words that exactly reflect the meaning of these three types of love.

When I say, "I love you because you are you," this is friendship. It is more than mere words, of course. I might better use the language of action. Love of friendship means: "I *do good* for you, because you are you." Friendship, however, is not the kind of love that underpins Fletcher's ethics. Morality extends beyond the circle of my friends. Romantic love means: "I do good for you because of my emotional and sexual attraction for you." One would think it obvious that such romantic sexual love is not a sufficient basis for an ethics. Situation ethics, however, seems to have been doomed to suffer this misunderstanding. "Love" in American parlance means romantic sexual love. An ethics based on love, therefore, translates into a permission for sexual license. "Love and do what you will" comes out to mean "follow your sexual impulses." Fletcher must take some of the blame for this misunderstanding since many of his illustrations are drawn from the area of sexual morality. He intends, however, to build his ethics not on *eros*, but on *agapé*.

Agapé is a love which extends far beyond friendship or passion. It is a universal, devoted good will. "I do for you, not merely because you are *you* (friendship) and not merely because I am emotionally or sexually attracted to you (passion); no, I do good for you simply because you are a fellow *human being* (universal love)." This love extends to enemies as well as friends; it includes those who repel me as well as those who attract. It is not selective as friendship is. It excludes no one as passion must. All human persons come into its ambit. Any action done out of loving concern for others precisely as human beings is a morally good action.

With an assist from the mass media, this situation ethics has managed to co-opt for itself the slogan and label of being the "new morality." How "new"? "New" because it is based on love rather than on external commandments; these latter are (supposedly) the basis of the "old morality," especially in the Christian moral tradition. Fletcher's ethics claims to be "new" also because it focuses on the uniqueness of each situation in which moral decisions are made; the "old" morality (allegedly) appeals to universal laws which are made to apply to all situations regardless of the particular circumstances involved. The two hallmarks of the "new morality" are (1) loving concern for others (2) in the unique situation.

The new morality thus claims to be an *intrinsic* morality. It flows from the heart and not from extrinsic commands. When confronted, for example, with the decision about whether or not to commit adultery, I don't have automatic recourse to the traditional prohibition: "Thou shalt not commit adultery." No, I have to face up to the demands made by the situation on my loving concern for others. Consider, for example, the plight of a woman in a concentration camp; suppose she can obtain her release and return to her husband and family if only she will sleep with the guard. The "old morality" says that she may not pay this price. It violates the commandment against adultery. The new morality requires that she consider the persons involved in the situation—the guard, herself, her husband and children. She must ask herself how she can best show her loving concern for all these people involved in the unique situation in which she finds herself. What decision will do the most good for all concerned? No universal commandment can do justice to this particular situation—*except* the command to love, which is the basis of the new morality.

No action, then, can be considered morally good or morally evil in itself, independently of the circumstances. Moral value lies not in the objective action, but in the subjective love which I show in performing the action. As for Sartre, what matters is *not* what I do, but *how* I do it. Sincere, authentic freedom was the *how* for Sartre. Universal, devoted love is the *how* for Fletcher.

So in principle, then, any possible action might be justified as morally good, *provided that* it is done out of loving concern. There are no *absolute* prohibitions or commands. Indeed it is hard to imagine how killing or rape or the seduction of young girls into prostitution can be manifestations of loving concern. However unlikely, the new morality can never endorse any action as good or bad in itself. It always depends—on the situation and on the love.

Love and Irrationality

Is Fletcher saying that love is blind? Is his ethics totally irrational? Is my moral life to be reduced to an attempt to live lovingly and in an absurd world that gives me no objective clues as to what is good and what is evil? No. This is not a world of Sartrean absurdity. A loving search for the other's true good demands that I use my intelligence. The consequences of my choices should be considered. The moral meaning of the situation is not totally created by me as Sartre would have it. The situation imposes its own demands on my love. But granting that love is not blind, once I have chosen it, then my act is unqualifiedly good. What may appear to be evil in itself is a loveless life which degrades both practitioner and client. But suppose that a woman has a choice between starving her children or resorting to prostitution. Her unique situation may dictate that she take to the streets as an expression of loving concern for her children. The old morality would say that this is an evil course of action, though maybe the lesser evil to letting her children starve. So her morally best course may indeed be to choose this lesser evil. The new morality refuses to qualify her choice of prostitution as evil in any way. She chose in loving concern with her eyes wide open. This love transforms what at best appeared to be a dubiously evil action into a moral good.

I personally wonder whether this sympathetic interpretation of the harlot's fate is as merciful as it appears at first blush. Such situational thinking appears to be progressive in its challenge to traditional norms and laws. But its strength may turn out to be its greatest weakness. Precisely because it focuses so narrowly on the uniqueness of the situation, it ignores the wider scheme of things. When the prostitute proceeds out to the sidewalks with the situationist's unqualified blessing, there is no *moral* reason for her to seek another or better course. Her decision is not the lesser evil. Love has made it good. So why would there be any moral reason for changing the social situation which reduces women to choosing between prostitution and starvation? Love is enough. No situation can be branded as objectively evil if the participants are coping with it in love. Unwittingly, situation ethics blesses the established order of things, the *status quo*, i.e., the *situation*! What appears to be a program for progress in morals can turn out in fact to be a philosophy of reactionism.

There may, I think, be a way out for the situationist. The whole question is: How wide is the situation? What is the philosophy of man underlying this new morality? Individual human beings are not islands of freedom in competition with each other as Sartre's philosophy would imply. Rather, for Fletcher, humankind forms a global society to be drawn together in the bonds of universal love. From this point of view, the *situation* of situation ethics comprises the whole human race! Such is the force of Jesus' teaching from which Fletcher draws his inspiration. But within this universal "situation" there are sub-societies, narrower societies within which I move and make moral decisions. "Loving concern" is all well and good, but how widely should my loving concern extend in any given case?

A couple in love might say: "It is for us two to decide whether to live together; we are concerned only with love, i.e., with doing the right and good thing for each other." Another couple might say: "Our families are involved in what we decide. We should consider their good as well as our own. Our loving concern extends to them too." Another couple might say: "Our decision about whether to cohabit affects the general attitude toward marriage of the country as a whole; we should not leave this out of our loving concern." A final couple might say: "Our decision about our own sexuality involves the very meaning of human sexuality in itself. In deciding for ourselves, we are really deciding, 'this is the way that human sexuality should be.' Humankind itself should not be excluded from our loving concern."

Agapé involves this final universal love. In principle, then, every moral decision based on such love involves a vision of mankind as large as the world. This would be a truly progressive and revolutionary morality. For it would aim at a universal human society united in a universal love. In its actual applications, however, the new morality hardly ever operates in such a universal context. The situations are much more narrowly circumscribed. And the narrower the situation, the greater is the tendency to acquiesce in the *status quo*, and what might have been a philosophy of revolution becomes an unwitting reinforcer of established evil.

So, contrary to the title of this section, it seems that we are left with the conclusion: "Love is *not* enough." The question always remains: Love whom? Love how many? All mankind? My nation? My church? My family? My spouse? The situation, to be sure, makes demands on my love. But how wide is the situation? How far do I accept the situation as it is? How much should I seek to change it from the viewpoint of a wider situation? Love alone cannot answer these questions, because love transforms any decision I make into a morally good decision, however widely or narrowly I define the situation.

Fletcher, I think, appears to end up with an irrationality in ethics almost as great as Sartre's. Sartre said that no situation outside myself could give me a clue as to how I should decide good and evil. In contrast, for Fletcher, the situation can act as a guide for my loving concern. But I have no guide to point out the guide. I have no way of deciding just which situation is to be my guide. So what started out to be an ethics based on mature loving response, seems to end in sentimentality, in mere feeling.

This conclusion would come as no surprise to the emotivist. The emotivist sees ethics as a matter of feeling. To think otherwise leads to nonsense and to insoluble philosophical problems. We have seen two approaches to morality that stress its irrational character—those based on the irrationality of Sartrean freedom and on the ultimate sentimentality of Fletcherian love. We look now to the case for an ethics built on feeling alone.

FEELING IS ALL THERE IS: AYER AND STEVENSON

Sartrean ethics flourished on the European continent, but never found strong roots in America. (We have a scientific bias against such extreme irrationality.) Emotive ethics is a British import. Unlike the new morality, its inspiration is strictly philosophical rather than religious, and the American philosophical world has given it a warm welcome. It springs from a typically British no-nonsense, down to earth analysis of why people fight about morals, and why disagreements about morality are so hard to decide. What kind of a language game is going on when people talk about moral good and evil? Notice that the question focuses on *language* about morals. The philosopher's job is to *analyze* that language and find out what's going on. This approach to philosophy, then, is called *linguistic analysis*.

Emotive Ethics

It is the conviction of these analysts that all philosophical problems, including the endless disputes about morals, are rooted in the misuse of language. It's not just that we don't know what we are talking about. We don't know what we are about to begin with. We're like the athlete who shows up at a bowling alley in helmet and shoulder pads with a football tucked under his arm, wondering where the goal posts are. He has his games mixed up. You don't score touchdowns in a bowling alley. So, too, the reason why we never seem to be able to come to definite conclusions in morals is because we've got our language games hopelessly mixed up. We think that we're playing one game when we are really playing another. As the psychoanalyst provides therapy for the confused mind, so the linguistic analyst sees himself as a therapist for the confused and muddled use of language. Let's look first at the tough-minded hard-line analysts.

The implements we play with in language games are *statements*. A statement is any group of words that makes some grammatical sense. Here are some examples: "The temperature is 50 degrees Fahrenheit." "The soul is spiritual." "God save the Queen." "Abortion is morally wrong." "Good heavens!" "Hail to thee blithe spirit, bird thou never wert." "Mercy killing is morally good." The following are not statements: "but and cow under"; "doogy how nimbus the"; "blitri sdfg oem2";—they make no grammatical sense.

With statements, there are two basic games we play, truth games and feeling games. Truth-game statements, say the analysts, are called propositional statements. Feeling-game statements are called emotive statements. Once we get the game rules straight, we can decide what kind of game is being played in ethics. Let's look at the truth game first, which is played with propositions.

Propositions are statements which claim to be true. Some of them I *know* to be true because I can prove them: "The sun rises in the east"; "the moon's gravitational attraction causes tides"; "2 + 2 = 4"; "a bachelor is an unmarried male." Other propositions that I know to be false are: "The sun rises in the west"; "7 + 5 = 13"; "it never snows during the winter in Buffalo." Finally, there are propositions that could be either true or false. I need more evidence before I can be sure: for example, "The value of pi is 3.1415342"; "there are volcanoes on the planet Pluto"; "the Cleveland Browns have a better ground game than the Chicago Bears." *You* might know whether these last propositions are true or false. Right now I don't have the evidence. But the point is that some day, in principle, evidence may be supplied to prove them either true or false. I can discover the value of *pi* if I learn and apply the proper rules of mathematics. We can learn about the volcanoes on Pluto when a rocket with cameras can be sent near enough to photograph it. The year-end football statistics will help me decide which team has the better ground game. All of these statements are in the "true-or-false" ball park. It makes sense to ask whether or not they are true, because I have a definite way of deciding. Some things can be proven true using my mind alone: They are true by definition ("A bachelor is an unmarried male") or mathematical logic ("2 + 2 = 4"). Other things need to be empirically verified as true or false. I need to use sensible observation to decide about the weather in Buffalo or the volcanoes on Pluto. Logic and scientific observation are the two ways of playing the truth game. Let's look now at the feeling game, and then we can decide what the analyst does with ethics.

Probably most of our statements express feelings rather than truths. Consider the following emotive statements: "Hi! How are you?" "I dream of Jeannie with the light brown hair!" "I think that I shall never see a poem lovely as a tree." "Existence precedes essence!" "The soul is spiritual." You have to admit that it would be pretty silly if someone came up to you and said, "Hi! How are you?" and you answered "That's true," or "That's false." Such a greeting simply isn't in the truth game. It's not true; it's not false. Rather, it expresses a feeling. It signals a positive recognition of a friend or acquaintance. Similarly the line from Joyce Kilmer's poem, "I think that I shall never see a poem lovely as a tree," is intended to express a feeling, not a fact.

However, statements such as "the soul is spiritual" or "abortion is morally wrong" are more tricky. These apparently are stating facts. They *seem* to be part of the truth game. We are fooled by appearances, says the linguistic analyst. Take a closer look at the statement: "The soul is spiritual." There is no possible experiment on earth that could ever prove or disprove this statement. In its grammatical form, "the soul is spiritual" looks like "the temperature is 51°F." But I can test the truth of the latter by checking a thermometer. There's no way I can test the truth of the former. So, though it looks like a truth-game statement, it really isn't in the truth game at all. At best, it expresses a feeling. It makes me feel religious or godlike, for example, to say that the soul is spiritual. But when I go on to say that it is more than a feeling—it's a fact—then I'm talking nonsense. That's why if you get into an argument about whether the soul is spiritual, the argument can go on forever. You might think that you're debating a fact, but what you really have is a conflict of feelings that cannot be settled by procedures such as looking at a thermometer, taking a pulse or running a formula through a computer.

All of which finally brings us to the emotivist way of viewing ethics, namely, that ethics belongs to the feeling game. Once again, the linguistic analyst tells us, we are deceived by appearances. Ethical statements look like statements of fact. "Abortion is wrong" looks like the statement "the ocean is wet." The difference between them is this. I can readily prove to you that the ocean is wet by pushing you overboard, but there is no experiment that I can possibly devise to show that abortion is morally wrong. Basically it's a matter of taste. I could argue for hours with you about whether a striped tie is more becoming to a particular shirt than is a plain tie. There is no way of settling the argument. It's a matter of private preference or taste. I could argue for hours with you about whether or not abortion is morally wrong. There is no way of settling the argument. Basically it concerns your private sense of morality. I *feel* one way about it. You *feel* another way about it. We think that we're playing the truth game, and so we fight on and on, but we're really involved in a feeling game, so the dispute can never be settled (except perhaps by a fair fight!). It's my preference against yours.

Attitudes Cause Beliefs

The upshot of all this is that you can never call a moral statement true. Nor can you call one false. It's just not in that ball park. When people forget this, as they usually do, they are simply allowing their moral feelings to masquerade as facts. And so they get hot under the collar, talk nonsense and argue in endless circles. One thing they never do is settle the truth of anything. And the reason is that truth is not at stake. In morals, the question is not who is right, but whose feelings will prevail.

Indeed, the analyst continues, this language of feeling finds its way into popular talk about morals, especially among the young. "I feel that moral decisions should be left up to the individual," is the universal refrain and cliché. "I feel that premarital sexual intercourse is good if there is no harm done to the other." "I feel that euthanasia should be legalized." "I feel that all war is immoral." "I feel that busing to achieve racial balance is morally wrong." And so it goes.

This emotive ethics leads to that other refrain of "do your own thing." I feel that my way is right. Why? I feel it and that's enough. My feelings are self-validating. Morality, then, is nothing but the indefensible set of feelings I have about preferred or rejected behavior. You must respect my feelings simply because they are my feelings.

I'll respect yours. Why? Because I feel you should respect my feelings.

Such an emotive approach, of course, leads to extreme rela-
tivism. There are as many moralities as there are people. And there's
no way of telling whether one is better than another. Indeed, they are
all of equal merit in that they all have the same basis—the individual's sincere feelings. As the emotivist has pointed out, it is nonsense
to pretend that any set of moral feelings is *truer* than any other. We
are not in the truth game here. Feelings are not true or false. They
just *are*, period.

What is to be said about this emotive theory of ethics? I personally would be hard put to deny that there is a large dose of feeling
that goes into my moral beliefs and behaviors. It is no surprise, for
example, that a hyper-emotional atmosphere envelops the legislative
assembly chamber when legislation about abortion, euthanasia, or
even war is discussed. Nor are we surprised at the mutual recrimina-
tions when morality attempts to bridge the generation gap. My moral
life is no mere objective, intellectual exercise of looking for the right
answer as if I were totaling up a grocery bill. My moral life is a commitment whereby I put myself on the line in mind, body, feelings, action—all that I am. When you challenge my total person, my feelings
jump to the defense of the human moral commitment I have made.

And so when I question my daughter's moral judgment concerning her relations to her boyfriend, I am in fact attacking the moral
personality that she is shaping by her decisions. It's not merely like
pointing out a mistake in multiplication. It's as though I'm putting
the finger on her flaw as a human being. And her emotions will
respond accordingly. Or again, when the representative argues for or
against legalized abortion in the state assembly, his arguments become soaked and heavy with feeling, and provoke an emotional over-
kill in the opposition's response. Proponents of legalized abortion
become "murderers" and opponents "cold and calloused to the plight
of women." No longer does the argument turn on the merits of the
case, but rather on the very right of the debaters themselves to be
viewed and treated as human beings. For morality is the measure of
your worth as a human being. (Recall our definition of moral good at
the beginning of this book: That action is morally good which is
faithful to what it means to be a human being in all that that involves.) In attacking my morals, you attack me, and my emotions
respond accordingly.

So whatever may be your final judgment on emotive ethicians,
they have a deep and true insight into the irrational side of morals

and into the important role played by feelings in the moral life. Morality is no antiseptic intellectual game played by objective uncommitted participants. It is an emotive game in which the players are totally committed. The stakes are nothing less than their worth as human beings.

In the end then, I would say, the question is not whether feelings are important, and at times even decisively important in ethical decisions. Feelings are there, and they are there to stay. And we really wouldn't have it any other way. These feelings are valuable. They are the signal of how deeply we are committed as human beings to the great goal of our moral living which, as Sartre stressed, is to shape the meaning of our lives on earth, to create for ourselves a human essence, in the image of what each one believes it means to be a human being.

The only real question that remains is: "Are feelings all there is in the moral life?" Are morals merely a matter of subjective taste? Is it really the case, as the emotivists claim, that truth has nothing to do with morals? The consequences of a "yes" answer to these questions are pretty hard to swallow. I find it hard to believe that the good or evil of a moral policy of genocide is simply a matter of how my feelings have been psychologically and sociologically conditioned to react to genocide. If I remain on sheerly emotive grounds, I'd have to conclude only that what satisfies a Hitler's moral sensibilities offends mine, and that's that. Nothing more can be said about the good or evil of the genocide of the Jews in Nazi Germany. Again, on sheerly emotive grounds, the man who deserts a faithful wife and loving children is the moral equal of the man who sees his family through sickness and poverty, faithful to his marital commitments. All that matters is that he felt good about his action. Feeling good makes it good. The moral feelings in each case are tremendously important to be sure. The moral feelings of most of us would be repelled by a policy of genocide. The moral feelings of many a man help keep him faithful to his loved ones though times are hard and temptation is strong. But are there not times when I have to say: "You may feel that is right; but it is not true; you are wrong"? In other words, does not morality involve the truth game as well as the feeling game?

Yes, say the ordinary language philosophers. Ethics is a matter of beliefs (the truth game) as well as of attitudes (the feeling game). There is another brand of linguistic analysis called ordinary language analysis. The conclusions of extreme emotivism offend common sense, say the ordinary language analysts. If you want to find out what ethical statements mean, i.e., what kind of language game is going on, don't ask professional philosophers. Ask the man in the street. Or at least, listen to him talk. Find out what kind of game he is playing. Don't tell him what kind of game he ought to play. The professional philosopher might think that there are only two ways of playing the truth game, i.e., by using either the rules of logic, or the rules of the scientific lab. But the man in the street knows better. He is convinced that his ethical beliefs are a matter of truth and not merely a matter of taste. He will admit that he cannot prove them mathematically or in the scientific lab. But they are true nonetheless, he asserts. The ordinary language analyst takes seriously this claim by the man in the street. He concludes that although the truth game in morals may not follow the rules of logic or of laboratory science, still it *is* a truth game, and it is played according to its own rules. Ethics, then, should not be reduced to mere feeling. Along with my moral attitudes (i.e., feelings) there are moral beliefs (i.e., assertions of true or false) to be reckoned with.

The upshot is that I am not talking nonsense when I condemn a moral policy of genocide as a false and bankrupt course of action. The policy of a Hitler offends not merely my emotions (the feeling game) but my mind as well (the truth game). My attitudes or feelings are repelled by his actions and my beliefs stand opposed to him as well. I not only *feel* that genocide is wrong, but I *judge* it to be wrong. Or if I, as an irresponsible husband, abandon my family, I'd *judge* myself to have acted wrongly. There would be guilt feelings, to be sure. But those feelings would have a basis in fact. I'm wrong to abandon my family, not merely because I have been conditioned to feel that way, but because it is somehow wrong in itself. There is a sense in which marital fidelity not only feels right, but is true. There is a sense in which genocide not only feels wrong, but is false. Morals involve beliefs (truths) as well as attitudes (feelings). And they are intimately related to each other. It is the mutual influence of beliefs and attitudes on each other which distinguishes the moral truth game from the truth games as played in logic and science. This is how the ordinary language analyst sees the morals game.

First, attitudes affect and influence beliefs, often crucially and decisively. This is the irrational and emotive side of the ethical truth game which the emotivist sees so clearly. When the four-star general discusses pacifism, he brings more than logic to the conversation. His emotive attitudes will profoundly shape the way he judges pacifist beliefs, evidence and arguments. And when a sexually aroused teenage boy attempts to persuade his reluctant girl friend to conform to a liberal sexual ethic, the activity of his hormones and the coursing of his blood will ensure that his beliefs and the evidence he offers are less than completely rational. In the morals arena, unlike the mathematician's study, *attitudes affect beliefs*. My feelings affect the shape of what I consider to be true. But feelings are not *all* there is. Truth *is* involved. Attitudes affect beliefs, but the converse is also true.

Beliefs affect attitudes, often crucially and decisively. This is the rational side of the ethics truth game which is glossed over by the emotivists. I can bring to bear evidence to back up my moral positions. Moral convictions are neither mere whims to be decided by a toss of the coin, nor the result merely of a blind conditioning process which is impervious to all rational criticism or reasonable evaluation. I can look at my moral feelings and ask if they are reasonable. I can defend on rational grounds my moral decisions to those who would criticize them. A problem drinker, for example, with a strong overlay of alcoholic attitudes may with great emotion defend the alleged therapeutic effects of ethanol in his life. But if his doctor shows him charts of how his brain, liver and nervous system are being damaged by alcohol, and if he sees a friend die of cirrhosis, and if he goes "on the wagon" and his sex life improves, he may well change his moral attitude about drinking. Beliefs (i.e., truths based on evidence) can affect attitudes. I need not consider myself condemned to follow an irrational set of moral attitudes in ethics. My attitudes are influenced by reason. Beliefs backed up by evidence can make a difference. I personally would concur with the ordinary language analyst that ethics is a matter of mind as well as of heart.

What my mind sees can change even deeply held ethical feelings. I know of a young military officer, for example, who was making the army his career. But after a firsthand battlefield experience of the indiscriminate slaughter that is part of modern warfare, he terminated his career on moral grounds and became an ardent pacifist. Again, I know a dedicated Roman Catholic clergyman who, after doing social work with bewildered pregnant teenagers, with their attempted suicides and recourse to quacks, began to see the wisdom of legalized abortion. And for a final example, the experience of family responsibilities can modify the liberal sexual ethic a man might have held as a bachelor.

Note that in each case the change in ethical conviction involved both beliefs and attitudes. There was new evidence for the mind (the events of the battlefield, the emotional and physical traumata of the pregnant teenagers, and bills and hungry children). Each case also involved an emotional jolt to challenge attitudes previously complacently held. The moral life involves the whole human being. An ethics of feeling alone is not enough. Ethical decisions reflect the blend of rational and irrational that makes up every human being.

CONCLUSION

Well, if ethical decisions involve my mind as well as my feelings, how do I go about using the mind to solve moral problems? What exactly are the rules of the ethical truth game? Can they be codified the way the rules of the logic game are codified? The young mathematician can be trained to follow clearly stated mathematical rules; the young scientist can learn the discipline and procedures of the lab. But granting that truth is involved in morality, how do I set about discovering that truth. Can the laws of ethical thinking be codified? It seems not.

I can prove that two and two are four, but it seems that I cannot *prove* that abortion is morally wrong. Feelings are not involved in arithmetic. But in morals, feelings cloud the truth picture. I am willing to call my moral decisions *true*. There are indeed reasons. However, the action of the mind is bound up with the heart. Ethics in this view is a matter of intuition rather than of strict logic. The heart has reasons which the mind knows not. This is the position of the ethical intuitionist. Attitudes and beliefs are merged into one activity. Moral good and evil are objects of intuition.

The moral life, then, might best be described in the language of myth rather than in the language of logic. The intuitionist trusts his inner moral sense to keep him in tune. "To thine own self be *true*," is his watchword. The touchstone of morality is within. But this "within" is trustworthy because it is in tune with the world "without" and the path along which my moral evolution is taking me. It is not the "within" of arbitrary emotions or of Sartrean freedom. These are blind. But there is a mental side to intuition. It *knows*, although it does not know *logically*.

The moral life is an *odyssey*, but it is not the odyssey of the ancient Greek epic in which Ulysses seeks to find his way back to his familial home. Conventional morality is best expressed by that ancient myth of return to parental ways. Intuitionist ethics rather is a modern myth of a moral journey as expressed in the movie *2001: A Space Odyssey*. One's goal is not clearly defined. But his inner moral voice propels him toward that unknown goal. If he is faithful to that inner intuitive voice, he will be transformed, reborn into the person that he is destined to become.

Such an approach is not so much a morality as it is a way of living beyond morality. There is no moral calculus of good and evil. One operates, to use Nietzsche's phrase, "beyond good and evil." The vision is mystical rather than logical. It more properly describes one who has arrived rather than one who is struggling to find the path. The final chapter, "Beyond Morality," will deal with this more at length.

In conclusion, we have so far stressed morality in its irrational dimensions. Morality has been viewed as flowing from blind determinism, absurd freedom, loving hearts, or irrational feelings. In the last chapter we saw Sartre and Wheelis challenge the psychological and sociological moral determinisms described in Chapter Three. And in this chapter, we have seen how difficult it is not to challenge the irrational subjectivity of an ethics based on love alone, or on feelings alone.

Situation ethics had said that love is enough. Moral good is whatever I do out of loving concern for others in a particular situation. However, we saw that love cannot dispense with intelligence. The question remains: Whom should I love? How wide is the situation that I should take into account? If love means doing good for the other, what is to be the test of this good?

Emotive ethics had said that feeling is all there is. Moral good is whatever I have been conditioned to feel good about. It has nothing to do with truth because there is no way to test it logically or verify it scientifically. But we saw that however important feelings are to moral decisions, the mind does make a difference. Beliefs and attitudes influence each other and the resulting moral intuition discerns good from evil, says the intuitionist.

Intuition, however, defies all logic and testing. It may not be irrational, but it is transrational. It operates beyond reason. It characterizes the moral life of the saint rather than the seeker. Those of us who tread more prosaic paths need a method in our madness. We can't always trust our intuitions. We sense that our inherited guilt feelings are not a sure guide. And we know how hard it is to love well. In a word, we need to use our minds. It is intelligence which can appraise our moral feelings, direct the path of love, and test our intuitions. Admitting the all-pervasive irrational side of morals, we look to reason as well. So now we proceed to the next chapter called "Mind-Power Morality."

SIX:MIND-POWER MORALITY

Nature binds truth, happiness and virtue together as by an in-dissoluble chain.

Marquis de Concordet

All nature is but art, unknown to thee;
All chance, direction, which thou canst not see;
All discord, harmony not understood;
All partial evil, universal good;
And spite of pride, in erring reason's light,
One truth is clear, Whatever is, is right.

Alexander Pope

There is no sin except stupidity.

Oscar Wilde

Mind-power morality puts intelligence at the center of the moral life. Ethics is mainly a cognitive exercise, not an emotive one. In the words of Oscar Wilde quoted above: "There is no sin except stupidity." Cognitivism in ethics rests on a long philosophical tradition going back to Socrates' injunction: "*Know* thyself." This approach finds its most persistent and perennial expression in the doctrine of natural law. Even in modern times, men look to nature as a guide to morals.

The contemporary concern for ecology is in a way a modern translation of the perennial concern for nature. Irresponsible tampering with the ecological environment (or with nature) does not go unpunished. Nature (the ecology) has its laws, and the intelligent and therefore moral human being will try to discover and respect these laws. There is a natural law, then, which is the mind's guide to morality. "Nature binds truth, happiness, and virtue together as by an indissoluble chain" (Marquis de Concordet). Of course, the meaning of natural law will shift and evolve according to how man's view of nature and of his own relation to it shifts and evolves.

The chapter begins, then, by comparing the pre-scientific and the post-scientific views of nature. The shift in focus provoked by modern science radically affects the way nature is to be used as a moral guide. Then we will describe two contemporary versions of mind-power ethics. The first is called objectivism. It is the right wing *laissez-faire* approach to ethics proposed by Ayn Rand.[1] The second is pragmatism. This is the liberal scientific approach to morals whose best-known proponent was John Dewey.[2]

THE NATURAL LAW

In the not too distant past, Christians (especially Roman Christians) were quick to defend their moral convictions by appeals to "the natural law." Implicit was the assumption that any man of good will who used his head to look at the natural order of things would arrive at these Christian moral precepts. Basically, these precepts were not to be considered peculiarly Christian, but rather a common human heritage. These moral laws were supposed to be written in nature itself for man's intelligence to discern and follow.

Reading the Book of Nature

It all seemed simple enough. God made nature a certain way. He made it that way because he wanted to make it that way. Hence to learn the laws and purposes of nature was to learn the laws and purposes of God. For example, it seems obvious that human sexual faculties were made to procreate children. We know this because this is what they do when we use them and do not interfere with their functions. If God did not want them to function for this purpose, he would not have made them that way. Therefore, since birth control is against *nature*, it is against the *law* of God. In a word it is against the *natural law.*

Natural law was not invented by the Christians, however. It is an inheritance from the ancient Greeks who looked upon the universe as an ordered harmonious whole, a *cosmos.* They noted the succession of the four seasons, the orderly course of the stars and the planets, the tides, the phases of the moon, the sun's daily procession across the sky. They asked themselves whence comes this cosmic order. Governments pass intelligent laws to order the actions of their citizens. In the same way, it seemed to the Greeks, the processes of nature seem to be ordered by an intelligent law. Aristotle viewed nature as the work of an intelligence. For the Stoics, every man's mind was a miniature reflection of this cosmic intelligence. So now "to act according to nature" means "to act according to the supreme intelligence." Man's mind is in tune, then, with the divine intelligence as manifested in nature.

Christians had no trouble adapting to their own purposes this Greek model of the cosmos. St. Paul (Rom. 2:14) gave the crucial hint, namely, that the Gentiles do by *nature* what the Mosaic *law* prescribes: "When Gentiles who have no (Mosaic) law do by nature what the law prescribes, these having no law are a law unto themselves." God's eternal law is present and operating in nature, they said, and just waiting to be discovered. The order of the universe proved the guiding hand of divine providence, keeping the stars in their courses, ensuring that season would follow upon season, and that the species of bird and animal would continually reproduce themselves, each keeping in its fixed and proper place. Human intelligence had only to discover the ready-made order of nature put there by the divine intelligence. Having discovered this order, what better could man do than to follow it? For this order represented the divine mind and hence the divine will. Ethics was thus based on the natural law. This natural law ethics was completely in harmony with man's view of God, nature, and intelligence and represented the best thinking of Western philosophers for two thousand years.

Writing the Book of Nature

The rise of science, however, shattered this view of human intelligence, and the evolutionary hypothesis shattered this view of nature. In this new framework, nature is far from being finished, far from harmoniously ordered. Species are not fixed, not even the human species. Man evolved from other animals, and man is evolving still. Since man, society, and the world are changing, new problems constantly arise challenging man to find new solutions. The laws of human nature, society, and the universe are not sitting there waiting to be discovered. The world is evolving, and so is man. In fact, man himself is determining which way he will evolve. Genetic experimentation, for example, is on the threshold of being able to create a whole new human species. Man is now writing the book of nature with the alphabet of space exploration, population control, Telstar communication, and nuclear research. It's not that modern man does not want to obey the natural law. There simply is no passive nature sitting out there waiting to be discovered. Man is shaping nature to his own purposes. Intelligence has become man's instrument of creation and control.

To assume a ready-made, given natural law would undercut this whole project of modern science. Traditional natural law appears to rest ludicrously on the argument that "if God had intended man to fly he would have given him wings." In this same vein, one might wonder whether central heating is against the natural law if God made the winters to be cold. Or assuming that God made some people with a sugar imbalance which leads to diabetes and death, is it against the natural law to take insulin to interfere with the sugar-producing function of the body? Assuming that God made some women with very weak hearts so that further pregnancies would mean death, is it against the natural law to take pills to prevent further pregnancies? In a word, is nature a book for man to read, or is nature a book for man to write? The former or Greek view of nature will give rise to a very different morality from the latter evolutionary view.

For Greek nature, there can be unchanging moral answers. Nature is ever the same; the same moral problems keep recurring and the same answers hold true. But evolving nature keeps giving rise to new problems challenging man to work out new solutions. For Greek nature, God established an unchanging order so that the order of nature reflects the intelligence and will of God. The order of nature becomes the natural law. But an evolving nature is to be continually shaped by man in his freedom. Nature reflects the intelligent creativity of man as much as of God. To a great extent, the order of nature is a product of man's activity. There is no ready-made natural law.

In Greek nature, the only change in natural law is a change in man's mind when he discovers something he didn't know before but which was there all the time. In the evolutionary view, not only man's knowledge changes, but nature itself is changed by man's knowledge. In Greek nature the moral law is discovered in nature. Nature is a book written by God to be read by man. Evolving nature is a book written by man; his only guide is his own moral responsibility as he tries to develop fully what it means to be an intelligent, free and social human being. One might imagine God patting man on the back, encouraging him to use his freedom with confidence and responsibility, but God is certainly dead as far as giving step-by-step answers and directions for the use of freedom.

The Greek view of nature and of natural law has become an anachronism in the scientific age. It died a natural death. Symbolic of that death was the failure of the Roman Church's last ditch effort to outlaw contraception on the grounds that it violated such a natural law. In matters procreative as in other areas of life, modern man shapes the course of nature rather than letting nature take its course. Nature is no longer king. Man sits on the throne. But there are signs that this seat is more precarious than he thought. A natural law backlash is in the making.

Our ecological problems give us due warning that we cannot rewrite the book of nature any way we like. There is still a sense in which nature's laws cannot be violated with impunity. Scientific control of nature must be tempered with respect. Nature teaches us that there are limits to human control. *Natura artis magistra*, says the ancient dictum. "Nature is the teacher of intelligence." This is the objective pole of the dialectic between man and his universe. This is the abiding kernel of truth in traditional natural law theory. This pole is the focus of Ayn Rand's philosophy of "objectivism." But nature is not absolute king. Nature submits to man. *Natura artis materia.* "Nature is the material with which intelligence works." This subjective pole stresses human scientific creativity and will be the focus of Dewey's pragmatic morality. Let's look in turn at these two modern versions of natural law.

OBJECTIVISM: AYN RAND

This fiercely independent, Russian-born American, Ayn Rand, is an anomoly—a lady philosopher! Hers is a morality that might be called an enlightened selfishness. Toward her fellow man, her policy is hands off, *laissez-faire*. Altruism is the source of all evil! Unconventional? Yes. We'll catch something of her spirit right off if we read her description of Kay Gonda, the heroine of one of her plays: "Kay

Gonda does not cook her own meals or knit her own underwear. She does not play golf, adopt babies, or endow hospitals for homeless horses. She's not kind to her dear old mother: She *has* no dear old mother. She's not like you and me. She never was like you and me. She's like nothing you bastards ever dreamed of!"[3]

"Ought" Is Based on What Is

What is the basis of this moral code that sees love as the root of all evil? Ayn Rand represents the exact opposite pole of thinking from the "will-power" moralities discussed in the last chapter. The focus shifts away from others and toward oneself: it is an ethics of "self-interest." And second, there is a shift away from emotions and will, and toward reason: it is a philosophy of *rational* self-interest. Mind, not will, is in the driver's seat.

Good and evil are not creations of the will (à la Sartre). No, good and evil are objective realities, and my mind is perfectly capable of discovering these realities. To refuse to use this mind is an immoral abdication of my humanity. So objectivism spurns moral codes that are based on revelation. There is something masochistic and suicidal about surrendering the direction of my moral life to a God. Such "altruism" is inherently immoral. Nor is a moral code to be based on subjective whim. Emotivists and existentialists alike are wrong in ignoring the fact that the world is perfectly rational. Moral good and evil are objective facts, not arbitrary whims, says Rand. Nor, she continues, should a moral code be based upon social tradition. Conventional morality, like revealed morality, is an abdication of my personal capacity and responsibility to use my own mind in guiding my life. For self-reliance it substitutes parasitism masking as "altruistic love." And we end up with mushy nostrums about the "evil of the profit motive" and the "need for a guaranteed annual income." This is a less than human morality that teaches people to live off the resources of others rather than rely on their own personal talent and effort.

Objectivism is a moral code based upon the objectively determinable principles of man's existence and survival. In the best Aristotelian tradition, it views man as first and foremost a "rational animal." Ethics is simply a matter of discovering the laws of my existence and survival and acting according to these laws. Morality is a code for survival. It's just that basic. The fundamental alternative in life is existence or non-existence: Swim or sink. This applies to all living things. Animals other than man automatically perform the actions necessary for their survival. But man has no innate knowledge of good and evil. For man, survival is a problem to be *solved*. Reason is the tool he has to solve it. Reason doesn't operate automatically. I can substitute for it revelation, feeling, or social conventions. In so doing, I would be abandoning morality by abandoning what it means to be a human being. Objectivism chooses to use this tool of reason, chooses to be the self-reliant kind of being that humans are meant to be.

Morality, then, is a code of values accepted by choice. A moral code embraces everything that I need for survival as a human being, i.e., as a rational being. From this follows the definition of moral good and moral evil. Moral good is that which is proper to the life of a rational being; moral evil is that which destroys the life of a rational being. The fundamental moral imperative of objectivism is quite simply "to think." Man must think, act, and produce the values which are required for the survival of his human life. "Thinking" is objectivism's cardinal virtue. Evasion, the rejection of reason, the suspension of consciousness (through the use of drugs or the practice of mysticism)—all these are manifestations of man's basic vice, the refusal to think. The good man is one who survives by his thought and productive work. The evil man is one who attempts to survive by parasitism, or force, or theft, or brutality. All these are attempts to survive irrationally by living off others. They are evasions of rational self-reliance. They lead to misery, anxiety, and destruction. They result in a society's ruination rather than survival and hence constitute the very definition of moral evil.

There is nothing mysterious about these principles of survival. They are based upon facts. Existence exists. The laws of life are staring me in the face. It is the mind's task to perceive them. This rational process is by that very fact a moral process. The initiative must be mine. Will I choose to undertake this rational moral path?

Reason, Survival, Self-Esteem

Objectivism, then, holds three values as supreme. The first is *reason*, the best and only human tool for survival. The second is *purpose*, our most fundamental goal in life, namely to exist and survive. And the third is *self-esteem*, based on the certainty that I am competent to think and worthy of living. Morality is not a luxury. Even if there were no God or no society, there would still have to be morality. It is a demand of rational self-interest. On a desert island you survive not by prayer or stringing beads, but by identifying facts and living in accordance with them. And this is morality.

What one *is* (one's philosophy of man) determines what one *ought* to do (one's ethics). It is this fundamental value of existence and survival that makes all other values possible. To choose against reason, against existence, against self-esteem and self-interest is the negation of all values. *Productive work* is the meeting place and supreme expression of objectivism's holy triad: reason-survival-self-esteem. The moral man is the one who chooses to exercise his mind fully in productive work.

Each person, then, is an end in himself, and not a means to the ends of others. True morality is egoistic. Self-sacrifice is immoral. In surrendering my basic self-interest, I'd be giving up the one value that makes all other values possible. Justice rather than altruistic love should govern my relations with others. Altruism is a morality of mere feeling, or irrational whim. I ask myself: What facts do your self-interest and mine require. There is no objective fact that requires me to give myself up to your desires or you to mine. Quite the opposite. I ask only the physical freedom to pursue my self-interest, and I give that freedom to you. To require more would be a contradiction. It could never be in the interest of the self to give up the self.

All men are not moral equals. Ayn Rand distinguishes between the worker and the bum, the murderer and the victim, the producer and the thief. Altruism's claim that neither wealth nor love needs to be earned is patent sentimentality. Love is not an alms. All men do not deserve it. Love is a moral tribute. It must be earned. Where altruism says: "I love you for what you are," objectivism says: "I love you for what you can become." It is the man who lives up to his potential, develops his mind and talents; he is the one who earns my loving respect. Altruism sees suffering as inevitable, reason as impotent, and hence makes of sacrifice a virtue. This attitude is immoral. It closes one's eyes to the victims of evil, to the predatory men who cause evil, and to reason, the pursuit of enlightened self-interest which can cure evil. Unearned forgiveness is a contradiction. One's enemies must earn forgiveness. There are laws of existence and survival that demand respect. To pass over them in a fit of sentimental altruism is immoral.

Clearly, *laissez-faire* capitalism is objectivism's ideal model for social morality. It is a misguided and immoral altruism for the state to interfere with the distribution of wealth. First of all, I have the right to live and pursue whatever values my survival requires, i.e., *life*.

Second, I have the right to think and act on my own judgment, without interference, i.e., *liberty*. Third, I have the right to work for the achievement of my own values and to keep the results, i.e., *property*. And finally I have the right to live for my own sake in the pursuit of my own personal goals, i.e., the *pursuit of happiness*. The alternative to these rights is a "cannibal society" in which men live off each other rather than by their own individual resources.

Government, in Rand's view, has one role only, to protect men from violence and fraud so that each has the physical freedom to pursue his rational self-interest. Socialist and Communist governments try to do more. In effect they encourage the cannibal society. They reward vice, the efforts of men to live off others. They punish virtue, the self-reliant men who are not allowed to keep the results of their intelligence and work. The whole society suffers from such misguided altruism. Leave intelligent and self-reliant men alone. If you do, you will share the benefits of their ideas. You will share in their minds. Ideas, after all, are free. Each man's first and only duty is to himself. If each could live out the truth of this maxim, the whole society would flourish. Each one could pursue what he wants and needs; he need not stand by helplessly hoping that others will give him what they think he wants and needs. I know what I want and need. My destiny is in my own hands. Virtue does not consist in placing my destiny in the hands of others. "Selfish" is not a bad word in this philosophy. "Selfish" is the highest good.

There is no doubt that Ayn Rand makes out a strong case to show that a morality must look to the good of one's own self. She rightly points out, too, the contradiction behind an unrestrained altruism that would urge love of others to the point of neglecting or destroying oneself. It takes a self-possessed person with a firm ego to make a good lover. To love means to give. A weak person who lets others parasitically bleed him dry will not long have much to give. A self-annihilating altruism is indeed a contradiction in terms as Ayn Rand well points out.

If the extreme of altruism does not do justice to the human situation (i.e., does not rest upon a tenable philosophy of human society), we might also ask whether the extreme of egoism is tenable either. I suggest that Ayn Rand in her stress on individual self-interest falls into an opposite error. Every individual person must be respected for his own sake as an *end* in himself. No one person should be treated as a *means* for another. This is the basis of her criticism of extreme altruism where the lover lets himself be used as a means for the cannibal beloveds. But does her egoistical philosophy in the final analysis urge that others be viewed as a means for fostering my own self-interest? Let's see.

For Rand, the fact that another person is in need does not put an obligation on me to fill that need. I have no obligation to impoverish myself by helping all the poor people in the world. So anything approaching a welfare state is an abomination to her. But the fact remains that I do not live on a desert island. I live in a world with other people. They gain from me and I from them. They are each ends in themselves just as I am an end in myself. In other words, each one of us is to be valued and respected precisely as a human being. Rand admits this in theory. Now what about in practice? How do I decide when I should help a person in need?

I should consult my rational self-interest, says Rand. What has the person in need done for me? Will my effort to help him receive a proportionate reward? The mere fact that he is in need puts no claim on me, even though I could easily help him without allowing myself to be bled dry or "used" as a means. The question is: What do I have to gain by helping him? This sounds to me very much like treating others as mere means to my own happiness, viz., others are worthy of my attention to the extent that they are useful to me. My love is not bestowed on human beings simply because they are human (i.e., as ends in themselves). No, my love is a tribute that must be earned. I love others to the extent that they contribute to my welfare, Rand implies. I love others insofar as they make it worth my while to do so. Isn't this saying equivalently that I view others merely as means to furthering my own self-interest?

If so, then I say that at this point Rand's philosophy breaks down. If other people (like myself) are truly to be treated as ends in themselves, as she herself maintains, then other people must have some claims on me beyond the merely utilitarian. One does not have to earn the right to be treated with the dignity befitting a human being. Every human being, insofar as he is human, is my equal. This gives him a right to my help, say, if he is starving and I have plenty. This makes me my brother's keeper. He does not have to earn the right to be my brother. As a fellow human being, he is already my brother.

Ayn Rand rightly stresses that merit as well as equality must govern dealings among men. The conflicting claims of merit and equality will be examined in a later chapter on justice. But if merit is all that counts, if you have to earn the right to be treated with dignity, then you are no longer being treated as an end, but as a means. Ayn Rand can't have it both ways. She wants to affirm that every human being is an end in himself. If so, then my egoistic island is inhabited by other people. In the pursuit of my rational self-interest, I cannot rationally ignore other selves.

PRAGMATISM: JOHN DEWEY

Ayn Rand stressed the objective pole of the dialectic between man and his universe—*natura artis magistra*—nature the teacher of intelligence. Nature teaches me the harsh facts of existence and survival. I must use my mind to discover these objective facts and live by them. Such is the moral philosophy called objectivism. But nature need not be viewed as man's unyielding master. Nature can be made to submit to man—*natura artis materia*—nature viewed as the material with which intelligence works. Human scientific creativity can shape nature to its own ends. This subjective pole of the dialectic between man and his universe will be the focus of Dewey's pragmatic morality. This is still a morality based on intelligence, but an intelligence which not merely passively reflects nature or the natural law, but actively changes it. Let's take a look at the world and the morals game through pragmatic eyeglasses.

"Change" is a key word for the pragmatist. Nature is not, as for Rand, rigidly and inflexibly proclaiming the stern laws for survival. Pragmatism is a child of the Darwinian revolution. The primary fact about nature, about reality, is that it is constantly evolving. Reality is process. Nothing just statically exists. All things are in a state of becoming or change. Clearly, then, any moral laws derived from nature will be open to evolution and change. Moral good will vary from age to age. What is good at one time could be evil at another. Pragmatism is a process philosophy. The approach to morality is no exception to this evolutionary standpoint of pragmatism.

Intelligent Actionism

The mind is not a passive spectator of the changing moral world, or a camera sitting by to record the passing scene. Another name for Dewey's form of pragmatism is instrumentalism. This is because he sees the mind as an instrument which I can use both to adjust myself to the changing world, and to change it where I can. *Pragma* in Greek means "action." Pragmatism is a philosophy of "*action*-ism."

The mind is what the mind *does*. What does the mind do? The mind is an active tool by which I cope with and change my environment. The moral man is one who uses this tool in the best possible way. It is this power of reflective intelligence that sets man apart from the other animals. The moral man is faithful to what it means to be a human being. And for Dewey, it is intelligent action that best characterizes man. Intelligence, then, is the basis for morally good decisions. Evil, for Dewey, is the refusal to submit my moral principles and moral decisions to the criticism of intelligence. It is an evasion of moral responsibility to rely blindly on tradition, on feelings, on authority, or to substitute rationalization for the scientific use of reason in my moral decisions.

Dewey is poles apart from Rand's atomic individualism. Everything, the individual moral agent included, can only be understood in its complete context. My whole social and physical environment defines me, just as I reciprocally take part in defining it. No man is an island. Nothing is self-sufficient. Everything is related to everything else. More technically, subjectivity and objectivity are mutually correlative. Experience and nature are defined by each other. Pragmatic philosophy is not an objectivism which sees only one pole, or an individualism that cuts man off from his whole surrounding and interacting context.

Again, this contextualism has its impact on pragmatic morality. An objectivist type moral decision made on the basis of consulting individual self-interest alone is unthinkable for the pragmatist. The human, and therefore the moral, situation in which moral decisions are made includes all the other persons and all the other circumstances that my decision cannot help but affect, and that in turn will affect me. Long before "ecology" became a cliché, the pragmatists saw that every moral decision was necessarily ecological. Every moral decision has ramifications beyond the individual decision-maker, on society and environment, and will provoke from these latter a corresponding feedback, and at times, backlash. To ignore this is unrealistic and unintelligent, and therefore immoral.

Recall the focus on *action*. Just as the mind is what the mind does, so I am what I do. I am, says the pragmatist, the sum of all my actions, processes and interactions. And obviously, my actions affect others, both persons and things. In the last analysis, my actions are always interactions. A self-enclosed individual agent is an abstraction. There is no such thing. Rand's rational, individual self-interest is inconceivable apart from the self-interest of every person my actions touch in any way, and indeed from the quality of the air I breathe,

the animals I enjoy, and the water I drink. Other people, the air, the water, the animals are all me. I cannot be, or be understood, without them. The pragmatist is akin to the Zennist here. The world is my body, says the Zen Buddhist. To be faithful to this philosophy of man, I must consult this body, this world, when I make a moral decision. For the pragmatist, the "self" of rational self-interest could be as wide as the universe. To pretend otherwise is irrational and therefore immoral.

This universe, in Dewey's form of pragmatism, does not include a transcendent God. In Dewey's expression, there is no place for the "supernatural." Christian theology's use of the word "supernatural" is different from Dewey's. "Supernatural" in Christian theology refers to what does not belong to human nature but comes rather as a free gift of God. "Grace" and "faith" would be supernatural in this sense. The soul and body would be natural. To have a soul is a natural part of being human, says the Christian, but faith is not owed to a human being: it depends on a supernatural gift of God. For Dewey, on the other hand, "natural" refers to anything that can be experienced. Whatever is alleged to lie beyond the realm of possible human experience Dewey calls "supernatural." And only the natural counts. Nothing exists except what can be experienced. Nature, for Dewey, comprehends the totality of human experience. This is why Dewey's philosophy is also called a "naturalism." That which is supposed to exist even though it cannot be experienced is "supernatural." Alleged supernatural "realities," in this sense, don't count, don't exist, however much misguided people talk and act as if these unobservable "entities" really existed. For Dewey, soul and God belong to this realm of the supernatural. They are beyond human experience, and therefore beyond the pale of rational philosophical discourse. Philosophy is concerned with anything that can possibly be experienced in any way, and that's enough.

So you will quite correctly expect Dewey's ethics to be naturalistic like the rest of his philosophy. "God" belongs to the realm of the supernatural. So you don't look to an alleged divine authoritative source of morality or of natural law. "Soul" would likewise be a supernaturalistic idea. So salvation of the soul or rejection of the material world in favor of the alleged spiritual are not valid human moral ideals. "After-life" also lies beyond the realm of human experience. Man has too long split his moral personality by opposing in dualistic fashion God's will to man's will, spiritual soul to material body, next life to this life. Naturalism heals this moral schizophrenia. The world of experience is the world where I live and move and have my being.

The progress of human society in this life is my moral goal. And man's will guided by intelligence is the best and only tool we have to achieve such moral progress. Dewey's confidence in human intelligence rests squarely upon the success of scientific intelligence.

Morality and Scientific Intelligence

Modern man has used scientific method with resounding success in the areas of physics, chemistry and biology. Man has even applied science to describe the development of human behavior in psychology and the patterns of social behavior in sociology. By science we have been able to describe and improve the material world. And we have even used science to describe the world of human behavior. But when it comes to the world of human *values*, the story is completely different. We haven't ventured a scientific attempt to criticize and improve the moral and social values by which we live. This is Dewey's diagnosis of the moral and social ills that plague us. Moral values have been considered to be too sacred to examine, immune from intelligent criticism, and sufficiently validated by tradition and past experience. It's not that efforts have not been made to critically re-evaluate traditional values. We've had, to use modern examples, the President's Commission on Pornography, the National Health Administration's study of marijuana usage, the Pope's Birth Control Commission. And with monotonous regularity, the conclusions of such scientific examinations of moral values are rejected in the name of unvalidated, blindly accepted tradition. When the chips are down, there is an almost fanatical resistance against examining moral values in an intelligent and open fashion. We exempt morals from enjoying the benefits of the most successful method that human intelligence has ever devised. According to Dewey and the pragmatists, our hope for moral progress lies in extending this method to our values as we have so successfully done in the other sectors of our lives.

Of course, we don't live our lives under laboratory conditions. Scientific method must be adapted and modified when applied to the area of moral decision-making. But the same basic process is at work with the same basic steps. When intelligence is functioning at its best, it unconsciously follows the rhythms of the scientific method. Recall that for Dewey the mind is a problem-solving tool. Thinking occurs when we have a problem to solve. Moral thinking occurs when we have a perplexing moral decision to make. As long as the organism goes humming along in tune with its environment, we are in the happy state of unproblematical experience—no thinking necessary. But there will inevitably come a time when we experience what Dewey calls a "felt anxiety." The need for a moral decision brings our happy evolution grinding to a halt. The decision-making process is triggered. Let's see how it works.

For the majority of us the decision is made blindly on the basis of habit or tradition, however inappropriate such a decision may turn out to be. The pragmatist calls this irrational, and therefore immoral. A past decision won't necessarily work in a new situation any more than a scientist's old hypothesis will explain new and unexpected data. So also if I am to act intelligently and morally (these are synonyms) I must examine my moral situation to determine what conflict is causing my felt anxiety.

For example, Guenivere is increasingly upset by her husband Bill's infidelity and failure to support herself and their three children. She has to make a moral decision about her marriage. Since she is a pragmatist, she will not automatically fall back on her Church's traditional taboo against divorce and stick it out no matter what. Nor will she blindly let things ride out of habit. A scientist carefully takes *all* the conflicting data into account. He would never get anywhere if he ignored the data that didn't fit conveniently into his theory. So too, Guenivere carefully considers *all* of the conflicting interest involved. The children have some love still for their father. Her own nervous health is breaking down. Bill's mistress is a gold digger and will probably drop him when she bleeds him dry. Any intelligent and moral decision must take *all* of these data into account.

If she were not a pragmatist, she might neglect her own health and stay together "for the sake of the children." Or she might neglect her children's feelings toward Bill, and walk out taking them with her, bound for parts unknown. Or she might file quickly for a divorce, ignoring the fact that Bill is being taken for a ride and that his bubble will soon burst. The pragmatist would call such decisions immoral, because they are only partial solutions. They don't take *all* the conflicting data into account. Like the genuine scientist, Guenivere, if she is to be moral, must come up with a hypothesis that takes into account all the aspects of her problematic situation, her own health, her children's feelings, her husband's behavior, his mistress' propensities.

When a scientist fails to consider all of his data, he's just being stupid. His solution won't work (the pragmatic test!). Whatever part of her problem Guenivere neglects will just come back to haunt her. She'd just be stupid. And for the pragmatist, to be stupid is to be immoral. So Guenivere must consider various hypothetical decisions that do complete justice to her problematical situation.

Pragmatism is a form of "situation ethics." And each situation is unique. The proper moral solution will vary from person to person and situation to situation. Guenivere, for example, might decide to file for divorce just to shock some sense into Bill's head. Or she might formally separate from him, keeping open the possibility of reconciliation after he becomes disillusioned with his mistress. Or she might divorce him, suing for support but assuring the children of visiting privileges. Although the possible solutions differ, the point is that pragmatism gives an intelligent method for deciding. First, like the scientist, I must make sure that my decision takes into account *all* the data of my moral problem. Secondly, like the scientist, I imagine the consequences of each possible hypothetical decision, and I pick the one that seems most likely to succeed in solving my problem. And finally, like the scientist, I test it in action. If it works, I'm back to my happy state of unproblematical experience. I have made a successful, intelligent, morally good decision.

But suppose it doesn't work? Like the scientist's experiment, the test of action will soon reveal the weaknesses of my hypothesis. The pragmatic method is no more infallible than is human intelligence itself. But the point is that this method is self-corrective. The test of action will show me how I have to modify my hypothesis, change my decision in order to make it work. If, instead of using this method of scientific intelligence, I make my moral decisions on the basis of irrational feeling or blind adherence to authority and tradition, then my moral decisions are much less likely to work, much less likely to be suited to the particular, problematical moral situation in which I find myself. And what's worse, feelings, tradition, and authority give me no method of correcting unsuitable moral decisions. I'm stuck with them. My only alternative is to flail about in the dark. The pragmatic method, on the other hand, is an intelligent self-corrective step by step procedure for moral decision-making.

Existentialists like Sartre have given "situation ethics" a bad name. Situation ethics has come (unfairly I think) to stand for arbitrary and subjective moral decisions, a kind of "anything goes" morality. Pragmatic situationism is not vulnerable to such a charge. It does justice to both the subjective and objective poles of my human and moral life. On the subjective side, it realizes that each person's life, situation and circumstances are unique. No universally binding, objective moral law can be laid down for all. My moral life, like the rest of life, is an evolving thing. But though nature (including my own human nature) is constantly changing, it has its own laws and makes its own objective demands. I can't get away with anything in my moral decisions. To be a human being, to be moral, I must above all be intelligent. The success of scientific method points the way toward the most efficient use of this intelligence. The pragmatist urges us to be bold enough to use the mind we have, to trust this intelligence, to follow this method wherever it leads. We need, he tells us, to apply the same open-mindedness and experimental method to our moral and social lives, that we have so successfully applied to the other areas of life. Nothing is too sacred to be subjected to criticism and improvement by the best instrument we have for human survival and progress, viz., the human mind honestly and openly regulated by the principles of experimental method.

CONCLUSION

The last chapter's look at the subjective moral philosophies based on feeling, will, and love was in this chapter complemented by a sampling of philosophies which centered on intelligence searching for a natural moral law. We thereby bring to an end our general reflections on ethics. We have shown in Chapter One how the determination of moral good and evil rests on one's philosophy of man. We examined the place of values and ideals in the moral life, and described in the second chapter the psychological stages in the moral maturing process. The next two chapters treated the determinism-freedom dialectic in morals. A moral code can seem like the confining walls of a prison when I see the psychological, sociological and anthropological determinisms that go to make it up. However, I need not remain the passive victim of these forces that shape my morality. I can step back and realize that they only have as much power over me as I give them. From this point of view, morality appears like a role I freely choose to play out on the stage of life.

This chapter and the last examined some of the moral scripts in the form of various philosophies of man underlying various approaches to the moral life. Emotive ethics, love ethics, and will-power ethics all put man on center stage as the creator of moral values. Natural law ethics and objectivism, on the other hand, put nature on center stage and advise man to use his mind to discover the natural moral law. Pragmatism attempts to unite these subjective and objective poles through the interplay of mind and nature under the discipline of the scientific method applied to morals. After thinking through these various alternatives, hopefully you will begin to get some idea of how you play the morals game.

Now comes the time to test your philosophy of man on some very concrete moral issues of our time. Racial justice, the sexual revolution, war and amnesty are all on scene to challenge your philosophy. But we will begin in the next chapter with the most basic problem of all—the moral issues surrounding human life and death.

PART TWO

PART
TWO

SEVEN: THE QUALITY OF LIFE

Laboratory reproduction is radically human compared to conception by ordinary heterosexual intercourse. It is willed, chosen, purposed, and controlled, and surely these are among the traits that distinguish Homo sapiens *from others in the animal genus . . . with our separation of baby-making from love-making, both become more human because they are matters of choice, and not chance.*

Joseph Fletcher[1]

Our technology has given us dependable machines and livestock; we shall have to choose whether to turn it now to giving us more efficient, convenient, and reliable men, yet at the cost of our freedom.

George Wald[2]

The past epoch was aimed at "Quantity of Life," i.e., anti-death, anti-disease, death-control, self-repression, and external restraint. The future epoch will be aimed at "Quality of Life," i.e., pro-life, pro-health, birth control, self-expression, and self-restraint.

Jonas Salk[3]

Experimentation on human genes and on human embryos, "test tube babies" and cloning, abortion, suicide and euthanasia, drug use and abuse—a book on modern moral issues cannot ignore these topics. Volumes have been devoted to exploring the complexities of each one on its own merits. Within the limits of only one chapter, we will have to concentrate on a single thread that unites all these areas of moral concern. Each involves a moral decision about how far one may legitimately exercise physical control over human life. Technology has raised possibilities hitherto undreamed of. We have drugs to shorten or prolong human life and to change its quality. Genetic experimentation is directed at mutating the human species itself. The medical ability to extend life has paradoxically raised the issue of when to mercifully end it—euthanasia. Not only mercy, but other reasons are adduced in favor of terminating embryonic life—abortion. Are there any moral limits as to how a person may shorten or even end his own life—drug abuse and suicide? Are there any moral limits on how human life should begin—test tube babies and cloning? In all these areas, two questions call out for moral clarification: (1) What is the meaning of "human life"? and (2) What are the moral limits of human "control" over human life? This, then, is the twofold theme of the chapter: human life and human control.

The first question directly relates to your philosophy of man. What criteria do you use to determine whether a truly *human* life is at stake? The second question will be largely an ethical consequence from your answer to the first. What moral guidelines should be followed in controlling, using, experimenting on, and terminating human life? The first section will consider three alternative meanings given to "human," namely, the sacral, the evolutionary, and the utilitarian approaches. The second section will consider three consequent ethical positions which we will call, in turn, the sacralistic imperative, the ecological imperative, and the technological imperative.

THE CRITERIA OF "HUMANNESS"

When does human life begin? What, indeed, is the foetus? The answers you give to these questions will provide the context for deciding the moral issues surrounding genetic experimentation and abortion. Is my human life completely my own to use and abuse as I choose? This question moves from foetal life to adult life. The answer you give to it will determine in large measure your ethical position on drug abuse and suicide. When does human life end? This question moves from mature humanness to the terminal stage of life. The answer you give to it will determine in large part your ethical position on euthanasia and organic transplants. So we will consider in turn the meaning of "human" as applied first to foetal life, then to mature life, and finally to terminal life.

Human Foetal Life

Under the umbrella of "foetal life" we intend to include all the stages of development from conception up until birth. At conception, i.e., when a spermatozoon fertilizes an ovum in the fallopian tube, an organism known as a *zygote* is formed. During the third week after the zygote reaches the womb and is implanted in the uterine wall, it technically becomes an *embryo*. Part of the tissue becomes placenta surrounding the other part which develops embryonically. Only after about the eighth week is it officially called a *foetus*. Until about the sixth month it remains an *inviable* foetus, i.e., incapable of surviving outside the womb. Then it becomes *viable*, and eventually (nine months) gets born.

So much for the medical biography. Now for the philosophical question: What is it a biography *of*? Do we have here the story of the early life of a human being? Or is it merely maternal tissue? Then the above story (let's call it, "I am Mommy's foetus") would be a story about Mommy and not about something human inside Mommy. Or do we simply have to admit that we honestly don't know anything about the human status of foetal life? This "know-nothing" school of thought has adherents representing both extremes of the spectrum of opinion about foetal humanness. We know nothing; therefore, play it safe; act as if it were human, say the conservatives. We know nothing; therefore anything goes; treat it like maternal tissue, say the radicals. However, is it really the case that we know nothing, that we have no clues at all about foetal humanness? It seems that such philosophical despair is premature. Biology has some clues for us.

Let's start by considering the zygote. At the moment of conception, what is created is a unique genetic package, with a chromosomal structure uniquely its own and differing from each parent's. So right off the bat we know we are dealing with an organism which in its biological structure essentially differs from the maternal tissue. Cell multiplication begins immediately as the organism develops in a human direction. This is the second fact we know. If all continues to go well, it will eventually develop into a human embryo, foetus, infant, and adult human being. It is not headed toward becoming a giraffe or an elephant. It has a human genetic code operative from the beginning. It is at least potentially human.

There are, however, in the zygote's eight day to two week life span prior to implantation some possible eventualities that would seem bizarre indeed if it were considered to be truly a human being at this early stage of development. Three biological phenomena stand in the way of granting the zygote full, albeit very young, human status. First there is the phenomenon of *twinning*. As has long been well known, during the first two weeks, the zygote can split in two, thereby creating identical twins. One organism becomes two. Secondly, and not so well known, there is the phenomenon of *untwinning*. What starts out as a double fertilization—i.e., non-identical twins—can combine into a single organism during that first two week stage of zygote life. Two zygotes become one. I do not say that two "human beings" become one. For surely even the most conservative definition of what constitutes a human being would include the trait of possessing a stable individual identity. This trait is not possessed by the zygote during the first days after conception. It would be a strange breed of human beings where two could become one and one could become two. Those who would insist on a completely human status for the zygote from the first instant of its conception would have to logically extend the full bill of rights to these erratically appearing and disappearing organisms. And the case would be all the more difficult for those whose definition of man includes the trait of possessing a spiritual immortal soul. They would be challenged to devise a plausible theory to explain the creation and annihilation of the immortal souls of these potentially very unstable, but hypothetically human, zygotes.

There is a final biological phenomenon which cautions against premature claims of full humanness for the zygote. It has been estimated that anywhere from one third to more than one half of successfully conceived zygotes never do succeed in getting implanted. In other words, at least one third of the zygote population never get to become embryos. They become part of the menstrual flow, dead before their parents ever knew they existed. Again, if you grant the zygote fully human status, you would have to conclude that one third of the human race faces the prospect of a most dismal and untimely end. (We'll leave it to the theologians to speculate what a boon this would be for the population of the limbo of unbaptized souls.) This, of course, is not a decisive argument. A high infant mortality rate need not imply that infants are not human, so neither need a high zygote mortality rate imply the denial of zygotal humanity. But two conclusions about zygote life emerge for sure. First, it's a tenuous hold indeed that the zygote has on existence. Second, and more problematically for its humanity, it is a very tenuous hold that the zygote has on its identity as a stable individual (this being the conclusion from its twinning and untwinning potential). On the side of the zygote's humanness stands the fact that it is a unique genetic package developing in a humanoid direction. But the phenomena just described would diminish the force of any argument in favor of granting to the zygote a full bill of human rights, or any argument claiming the presence of a human being (or a human soul) from the first moment of conception. This whole discussion has direct relevance to the moral assessment of birth control procedures which operate after fertilization but before the zygote's implantation in the womb (e.g., the so-called "morning after pill" recently approved by the FDA for public use, and possibly also the IUD or interuterine device). If the zygote is not human, then these procedures should be discussed in the moral context of contraception and not of abortion. In other words, contrary to the claims of some, they would not be abortifacients but contraceptives.

A zygote, once implanted, differentiates into amnionic tissue which forms a sac around the embryonic tissue. Now the embryo does have a stable individual identity: no more twinning and untwinning. And the possibility of miscarriage becomes more remote. It has a firmer grip on existence. As a stable individual evolving under the guidance of a unique human genetic code, it might, at least in some minimal way, begin to be construed as a human being. Indeed by the end of the fourth week, all the organs are present in rudimentary form, and the beginnings of eyes, ears, and extremities are visible.

The embryo is medically dubbed a *foetus* by way of celebrating its two month birthday. Rapid brain development has, by this time, made the head its most prominent part and external genitalia have appeared. And we could go on detailing the milestones of the foetus' journey toward adult humanness. The point of this chronicle is to demonstrate that we need not flail around in the dark regarding the question of whether foetal life is human. The "know-nothing" position simply isn't tenable. Biology does give us clues. Biology, however, can only describe the course of foetal development. What you conclude from such a description is incumbent upon your philosophical judgment. You may lack confidence in your philosophy, but don't hide behind the facade of alleged lack of data. The data concerning foetal development are just as clear as the data concerning the effects of alcohol on the human system. It is your responsibility to form philosophical and moral conclusions from such data. Our first conclusion, then, is to reject the "know-nothing" position, along with its moral conclusions of "play it safe" or "anything goes." Both conclusions are cop-outs. They are refusals to face and make responsible decisions regarding the available data.

A second conclusion is that biology makes very dubious any theory of human ensoulment at the very moment of conception. "When does the soul make its appearance?" To pose the question in this way is to put yourself in an either-or box. Either the foetus is human or it isn't. It all depends on whether and when the soul is present. This is a magic moment theory of human life. At moment "M minus one" there is no soul, no humanness. At moment "M plus one," after the advent of the soul, there is complete humanness. It all comes down to the answer to the unanswerable question: "When does the soul appear?" The question is unanswerable because, by definition, a spiritual soul is not observable. And so we are back to "know-nothing-ism"—but not quite. That magic moment, presuming indeed that such exists, cannot easily be imagined to occur before implantation. To insist otherwise is to take on the onus of concocting some bizarre explanations about the creation and annihilation of those souls involved with zygotal twinning and untwinning.

There is another way of approaching the data, a way which avoids both the "magic moment" and the "know-nothing" boxes. This is to adopt an evolutionary approach to the question of humanness rather than a soul-psychology approach. Humanness, in an evolutionary perspective, would not be a matter of *either-or* but of *more-or-less*. A growing, developing zygote with its unique genetic structure is more human than egg or sperm alone. An implanted embryo is more human than a zygote whose individual identity and hold on existence remain unstable. A foetus with brain and vital organs morphologically differentiated is more human than the young embryo whose chromosomal potential is just beginning to actualize. The viable foetus which could exist outside the womb is more human than the inviable organism whose survival depends on the uterine environment. The infant breathing and feeding outside the womb is more human than the foetus still physically attached to the mother. The child who speaks a human language is more human than the newborn infant who can only scream its desires without recognition. How long should we continue to mark the milestones on the way to achieving full humanity: puberty, marriage, parenthood, or shall we say with some existentialist philosophers that only at the moment of death does one achieve the full human personhood he has made himself to be? Anyway, you get the idea. The evolutionist does not latch on to some arbitrary magic moment or sign of humanness such as "the first moment of conception," or "when the embryo is implanted," or "when the foetus becomes viable," or "when the infant is born," or "when it shows human behavior like laughter or speech." "Human" is a matter of degree. There is a continuous line of evolution from conception until death. The ascertainable quality of the humanness involved enters into his moral judgments. An evolutionist would be more reluctant to abort a five-month-old foetus than to doom a zygote (say, by taking the "morning-after pill"), more reluctant to commit infanticide than abortion. Unlike the "magic moment" approach to humanness, in the evolutionary view there is a sliding scale of humanness, and a sliding scale of "rights" or moral consideration demanded by that humanness. It is not as clear-cut as the "anything goes" or "play it safe" philosophies, but it has the virtue of attempting to responsibly come to terms with the data as they are known.

Mature Human Life

A mature person (that proverbial "consenting adult") is undeniably human. Now the question shifts more from that of determining objective criteria for humanness (so controverted at the stage of foetal life) to determining subjective criteria for control over human life. Are there any moral limits to which the consenting adult should consent? The second part of the chapter will explore the alternative answers to the general question of subjective control as it extends to all human life. But *objective* considerations are not entirely irrelevant even to the question of *adult* humanness. A few of these we will now briefly outline.

Suicide is *the* test case for my understanding both of the objective meaning of human life and the extent of my morally legitimate control over it. Let's sample a range of philosophical options:

(1) *Extreme Subjective Utilitarianism:* I may use my life exactly as I please. My body is mine alone to control. This includes a right to suicide. There are no moral restrictions except in my own free decisions. This subjectivity is in the best Sartrean tradition and is exemplified in the *Humanist Manifesto II* which was signed in 1973.

(2) *Moderate Objectivism:* My body and my life are essentially involved with the bodies and lives of others. Therefore I have no absolute right to destroy them without considering the social responsibilities I have and the social consequences of such an act. Such a moral view might be reflected, for example, in a legal code which for-

bids suicide in general while permitting voluntary euthanasia.

(3) *Sacral Objectivism:* My body and my life are God-given gifts. I am morally free to control and use them responsibly. But I may never destroy them. Intelligent responsibility extends to every area of my life short of self-destruction. Traditional Christian condemnations of suicide and voluntary euthanasia rest on this philosophy of sacral objectivism.

(4) *Extreme Sacralism:* All life is sacred. Life in no sense belongs to us. It is a trust handed over to our charge. Gandhi's doctrine of *ahimsa* (non-injury to living things), vegetarianism, absolute pacifism are some doctrines which may flow from the extreme reverence for life.

Have you ever thought of suicide as an intelligent and morally viable way out for yourself or another? What do you think of people offering their bodies for dangerous medical experiments? Do you consider the use of harmful drugs as morally wrong for adults as well as for children? Closer to home, perhaps, are you presently practicing slow suicide by the excessive use of nicotine or alcohol, or by exhausting your bodily vitality in a job that is beyond your energies? Answer these questions honestly. Ask yourself which of the above four philosophical attitudes toward human life is reflected by your answers. This will prepare you to consider a life-and-death question in the forefront of contemporary moral discussion concerning life and death, namely, euthanasia.

Terminal Human Life

Difficulties of definition arise at either extreme end of an individual's biological span on this earth. First, there is the problem of defining death. The problem, in other words, of determining human life's inception is replaced by that of determining its terminus. Then there is the question of control (to be treated in the latter part of this chapter): Under what conditions is it moral to hasten or even cause death?

Ways of approaching the definition of death parallel remarkably those taken toward life's beginning. First, we have the unanswerable question: "When does the soul leave the body?" We don't know, i.e., we can't know: Souls are not observable. Therefore, play it safe. On this thesis, clergymen perform the "last rites" on bodies which have long since ceased to show vital signs of any kind. But we need not adopt an *either-or* (soul or no soul) approach. We can view the presence of life as a matter of degree, of *more-or-less*. The question then shifts to the *quality* of the life involved.

In this gradualist approach, if heart, lungs, and brains have all ceased to function, and decomposition has set in, then you are as dead as you can be. If, with the help of modern medical machinery, heart, lungs, and kidneys are maintained in function while the brain has ceased to function altogether, you're not quite so dead. There is biological life, to be sure, but human conscious functioning has ceased. If you are being wracked by pain in a certainly and imminently terminal disease, while only mechanical attachments keep you alive, you are not quite so dead. Your brain does function. But you are not quite so alive as a suffering imminently and terminally ill patient who is surviving without machines. If you are certainly ill of a terminal disease, but can be kept alive for some time by drugs and other therapies, you are more alive than one whose death is imminent. You get the idea. The evolution of human life from its conception in the womb is matched by its devolution. None of us is biologically immortal. Each one of us is terminal, although the nature of our own particular terminus has not made itself known as yet.

As we saw in the previous section, the way we use and abuse our lives has much to do with hastening or forestalling our end. So the classical question of euthanasia is only the limit and test case of making a moral decision to hasten or cause death. The decisions of our ordinary daily lives (e.g., about diet, exercise, and smoking) are in effect decisions determining the rate at which we are putting ourselves out of our misery. So clearly there is a perspective for which the hastening of the dying process, as well as the definition of death, need not be considered as an *either-or* proposition. As the end approaches, of course, such decisions become more dramatic and irreversible. Clergymen like to charge doctors with "playing God" if they hasten the dying process at its very end. But we should keep in mind that in all our daily decisions, we are "playing God" with our lives. Granting the biological devolution, the daily dying, that is an inevitable dimension of our adult living, doctors have come to a consensus about when human (as opposed to biological) life can be said to have definitively terminated. Human death in this ultimate sense is defined as the "absence of brain activity for over twenty four hours." This is the signal that irreversible brain damage has been done. There will be no more human-quality activity possible again for this organism. However severe the emotional wrench may be, there are few doctors, clergy, or families who would have any serious moral difficulty about terminating such a functionally non-human, machine supported, biological life. (The metaphor of "human vegetable" is often used to soften the emotional force of even this minimal death-dealing decision.) The more difficult decisions about euthanasia revolve around organisms in which the quality of life is not so minimal, i.e., when more than vegetable life-processes are involved, however attenuated or precarious these may be. And, needless to say, the less attenuated and precarious the hold is on human life, the more a moral reluctance will be felt about terminating it.

So we are now ready to move on from criteria of humanness to criteria of control. We noted similar approaches to criteria of humanness whether we were considering human life in its foetal, adult or terminal stages. The sacral (in general the Eastern Hindu-Buddhist or the Western soul-psychology approach) sees human life at every stage as an *either-or* affair. Moderate objectivism was more concerned with the quality of life than with its bare presence or absence. Human life here was defined on an evolutionary-devolutionary continuum according to its potential for individual use and social involvement. Extreme subjective utilitarianism sees nothing especially sacred about human life nor does it feel the need to accede to any particular demands arising out of the particular quality (or lack of quality) of the life involved. I am sure you have already begun to surmise the moral criteria for control that will flow from these varying criteria of humanness. It has been difficult to keep these two questions apart since the definition of human life is so closely bound up with its functioning and hence with the matter of control.

CRITERIA OF CONTROL

There are three moral "oughts" or imperatives that will yield us three alternative philosophies to guide us in the moral control of human life and death. These are (a) the technological imperative, (b) the ecological imperative, and (c) the sacralist imperative. We will describe them in turn, showing the kinds of moral reasoning each employs, and exemplifying some corresponding conclusions for human life and death.

The Technological Imperative

"Whatever science *can* do, science *should* do." This axiom sums up what we have called the technological imperative. The whole world is man's to control and improve the best way he knows how. Whether the universe is God-given or just plain given is irrelevant to this morality. There are no built-in moral limits to man's absolute dominion. Human life itself is a fit subject for his experimentation and presents the greatest challenge. And it is science which provides the most intelligent method we have of meeting this challenge. No taboos or prejudices should be allowed to hinder this unrestricted search for progress and truth.

In the case of adult moral agents, of course, consent should be sought for and obtained. However, granted consenting adults, technological experimentation should proceed unimpeded. But where the subjects are not morally responsible agents, even this moral limitation of "consent" tends to disappear. This is why discussion of the technological imperative tends to center around eugenics, genetic experimentation, foetal experimentation, and the more radical kinds of surgery and therapy on imminently terminal patients. In these subjects moral responsibility is absent or diminished, and technology tends to assume the driver's seat. A zygotal gene, for example, has no say about the lab technician's attempts to mutate it. A comatose terminal patient without relatives, or an aborted still living foetus, or a physically defective ward of the state all could and do function as unwitting objects for the technological imperative's imperious demands.

"Whatever science can do, science should do." Well, what *is* science doing? First, prenatal diagnostic techniques (like amniocentesis, for example) can detect gross chromosomal defects like mongolism and also can prenatally ascertain the sex of the foetus. Technology is now in a position to detect and abort incurable defective foetuses. In principle, now, only "quality" babies need be born. And for some, "quality" could mean the "right" sex (that male heir, or a girl to go with the boy you already have). A baby of the "wrong" sex need no longer be brought to term. Quality-of-life considerations combined with technological power make for pretty heady stuff indeed!

Second, technology can keep inviable, aborted foetuses alive for some days to be subjects, for example, of experiments on the effects of drugs on foetal life. Should these aborted foetuses be allowed to go to waste, the technologist asks, when experiments carried out on them could possibly benefit future foetal and human life?

Then there's parthenogenesis. Aside from artificial insemination in which the male contribution is separated from the sexual act, true parthenogenesis has been achieved in frogs and rabbits, i.e., the development of ova has been triggered without benefit of male sperm. Fur-

ther in the future lies cloning, i.e., the reproduction of identical replicas of individuals from a parental cell. Since technology *can* envisage
babies without sex, it *should*. The technological imperative justifies
morally the experimentation required on human tissue to bring these
results about, as well as justifying the results themselves.

The same moral justification is claimed for the development of
extra-maternal wombs. Some human embryonic growth has been ef-
fected in bottle wombs (the notorious "test tube babies"). Ovum
banks are being formed whence an infertile woman can have another
woman's ovum implanted in her own womb to be fertilized by her
husband. In the near future it is expected that a zygote will be able to
be implanted in a human womb, which will thus deliver a baby that is
biologically related to neither parent. This has already been accomplished with ewes and rabbits. The technological imperative justifies such radical tampering with the traditional idea of human parenthood.

Presupposed by this whole moral philosophy is that science is the
best tool we have for improving the species. This supposition is most
dramatically exemplified by attempts to mutate human genes, thereby creating different and presumably better species of humans as well
as chimeras or hybrid species. This would extend to mankind and the
higher animals what has already been accomplished with plants and
fruitflies.

This brief survey of some of science's goals for humankind might
well make you question the sufficiency of the technological imperative as a moral guide. There are no moral restraints or limits aside
from technological possibility. Do you choose to have it done? Can it
be done? Then do it! Such thinking has given us both ABC warfare
and nuclear power plants, organ transplant techniques, and the furnaces of Auschwitz—the Nazis, after all, were trying to improve the
human species. Such radical subjectivity might seem innocuous
enough in the context of a Sartrean insistence on each individual's essential loneliness in moral decision-making. However, extended to
technological decisions which will alter the species itself, such subjectivity takes on a more ominous tone in the view of this author.

The technological imperative brings us back to that world that
Marcuse warned of (see Chapter Three). Does technology exist for
man, or man for technology? Is it really true to say that what's good
for technology is good for man? Can we with impunity define man by
his scientific technology? The technological imperative presupposes
an affirmative answer to these last two questions. It has a close af-
finity to the subjective utilitarian definition of human life described in

the first section of this chapter. It is the kind of ethics that naturally flows from such a philosophy of man. Human life (be it foetal, adult or terminal) does not imply a *right* to life. It is not sacred in and of itself. What is sacred is the technological enterprise. To the progress of this enterprise human life must at times yield. This progress is self-validating. Taboos against eugenics or against foetal and genetic experimentation must not be allowed to get in the way. The right to progress must often take precedence over the right to life. One cannot assume a right to life from the mere fact that a human life is present.

The Ecological Imperative

To such radical technological subjectivity, the ecological imperative (as we have chosen to call it) introduces a note of what I would consider much needed caution and objectivity. Technology, this second philosophy asserts, cannot without impunity act with such brash independence or as though it were omnipotent. Man is more than his technology. And technology is beholden to man. Further than this, technology and technicians form but one force inextricably bound up with a universe of living and physical forces. Moral decision-making, then, should reflect this basic philosophical fact about man. Individuals function in systems. Affect the part and you affect the whole. No less than our fuel and water supplies, human life itself must be dealt with from an ecological perspective. The ecological imperative says that decisions about human life and death should not be made as if they had mere individual and subjective import. Individual decisions have an ecological backlash, like it or not. The ecological imperative, then, moves in the direction of a sacral and objective definition of human life. In other words, life is a force to be respected and not merely an object to be manipulated at will.

Genetic experimentation on humans, in this view, should proceed with caution. This is not to say that religious superstition or blind taboos should inhibit the scientist. Rather, the ecological imperative urges the scientist to act with his moral and rational eyes wide open to the consequences of his experimentation. He can't let himself off the moral hook by saying: "I just work here." A mutated gene is not merely a mutated gene. It could be the progenitor of a new species. A new human (or human-like) species is not merely a new species. It is a new life force that will interact beneficently or destructively with other (including present human) specific life forces. How would you, indeed, "improve" the race? Draw up a set of specifications for your ideal human. Do you have any presently living human candidates, the replicas of whom you feel should be cloned in large quantities? What kind of defects would you breed out of the race? Hitler had some pretty definite ideas on this point. This is not to imply that you couldn't do better. But it does warn that answers to these questions are not always so obvious. Breeding a race of ideal humans is more complex than breeding a species of ideal cows. Would you aim for intelligence—can you define it? Or beauty—can you define that either? It has been discovered, for example, that "retarded" women have the virtue of being able to take care of autistic children by the hour without getting bored. This is one talent you would breed out of the race if you eliminated such retards as "defective." Anyway, if the new race had an IQ of 200, would they lock up the 130 IQs as "defectives"? Even though technology *can* accomplish what it chooses, the ecological imperative questions whether it *should* do so. The impact of moral decisions on the whole life system must be responsibly taken into account.

The ecological imperative urges the same contextual approach to decisions about human foetal life, adult life and terminal life. Birth control, for example, seems like a good idea. And so does the ideal of prolonging the human life span. Put these two ideas together. Consider them contextually. Together, they represent a decision in favor of the old and against the young. Together, they are a decision to raise the average age of the human race. The ecological imperative urges us to take responsibility not merely for our decisions taken individually (e.g., for birth control and for prolonging human life), but collectively (i.e., to realize that the impact on the whole species is to raise its average age). Such ecological consequences come as a "surprise" to technology unimpeded, operating under its own imperatives. The ecological imperative tries to eliminate such surprises, and bids us to consider if this is really what we morally intend and choose to do.

This is not the place to try to outline the ecological implications of all the life and death questions mentioned in this chapter. We've seen briefly how an ecological approach to human genetic experimentation, birth control, and the prolongation of the human life span differs from an approach that is merely technological. Such universe-wide and species-wide considerations may seem beyond the ken of most of us. But the ecological imperative could also make us change the moral focus of our own individual lives.

As a final example, let us take an ecological look at what we called "slow suicide"—the neglect of health or the use of drugs. Such moral decisions about how I use and control my life can be considered on an individual moment-by-moment basis. Or I can consider them in the context of my life taken as a whole, in terms of *life-style*. The former approach is that taken by people who lament being so much overweight because they ate too much between the Christmas and New Year's holidays. The ecological or "life-style" approach says: "It's what you eat between New Year's and Christmas!" The ecological imperative, in other words, bids us to consider the impact of our decisions on our lives as wholes. The question is not just: "Will this cigarette hurt me?" or "Do I need this drink?" The question is rather: "Do I want to encourage a pattern of action that will impair my respiration and shorten my life?" "Do I want the kind of life where I turn to alcohol rather than to people for the relief of tension?" In the ecological perspective, a decision about part of my life is always a decision about the whole. As popular wisdom puts it: "He died as he lived." Suicide and euthanasia are decisions to foreshorten rather than prolong life. Less dramatic forms of the same decision are what we choose to do about exercise, work, relaxation, and drugs. The ecological imperative bids us to view human life decisions not piece by piece but in their impact upon all the life-support systems that sustain it.

The Sacralistic Imperative

The sacralistic approach to the ethics of human life and death is more conservative than the merely technological or even the ecological. The perspective is religious. As a divine gift (in the Hebraeo-Christian tradition) or as reality sacred in itself (the Hindu-Buddhist tradition), life commands absolute reverence and respect. Science may heal, but never destroy. In the Indian world, this applies to all forms of life. In the Western world it is *human* life which is singled out for special reverence. At the risk of being charged with "species-chauvinism," we will confine our remarks to this *human* level of life. But keep in mind that the sacralistic view rests on a fundamental faith in life itself to evolve spontaneously with a variety and quality that transcends any petty little ways we might dream up to "improve" it. Healing is favored. The medical arts help life to live up to its potential. Tampering is suspect. Life's potential is richer than our laboratory schemes. Destruction is tabooed. Life is an absolute value. Obviously there are problems here, and distinctions to be made, but this is the general thrust of sacralistic thinking.

It follows clearly that to actively destroy either a human foetus or a terminally ill human being is a *prima facie* moral wrong. But sacralists invoke a moral calculus to mitigate in varying degrees this apparently inflexible absolutism regarding human life. For example, if complications during pregnancy or birth pit maternal life against foetal life, moral space might be made for therapeutic abortion. Again, in the case of euthanasia, a distinction is made between passively letting someone die and actively putting him out of his misery. Extraordinary means might be appropriate to keep someone alive who has hope for a useful human life. But a patient who is suffering and terminal might have his death hastened by withholding extraordinary measures that could prolong the inevitable. And so the calculus works, balancing the utility and quality of the life over against the radicalness of the measures taken to prolong it. This principle of "not killing" but "letting die" is applied to foetal life as well. A pregnant woman, for example, with a cancerous womb might have the womb removed. Her life is saved. The foetus is "allowed to die." But the crucial sacralistic moral principle is maintained: The foetus was not—may not be—actively "killed," any more than may be a patient who is terminally ill.

A similar calculus is applied to the moral use of adult human life. Alcohol, nicotine, exhausting work—all these have good effects and bad. They can shorten life. They can also bring pleasure and accomplishment. And so the sacralist balances the good against the bad and makes his moral judgments accordingly. He is willing to balance life against life if need be, good effects against bad, and the hope for life against the means taken to prolong it. But direct and active killing (be it by abortion, human foetal experimentation, suicide, or active euthanasia) is a moral line the sacralist will cross reluctantly if ever at all. Indeed the conservative sacralist is concerned not merely with the taking of life but with all scientific interference with the natural reproductive processes. Birth control, for example, is not to be undertaken lightly. All human fertilization and development are to be the fruit of the interpersonal act of love, and not matter for impersonal laboratory experiments. And so a whole range of procedures from artificial insemination to experiments on human genes are liable to his condemnation as insufficiently respectful of human life.

The sacralistic moral calculus often seems like rationalization rather than reasoning. The distinction, for example, between *killing* and *letting die* can become pretty fine, and at times seems to verge on the purely verbal. Consider an ectopic pregnancy, in which the embryo is implanted and developed in the fallopian tube instead of in the womb. It cannot come to term. The sacralist says to snip out that section of the tube and thereby allow the foetus to die. Is this "killing" or "letting die"? Nor is the distinction always so clear between active euthanasia, which the sacralist condemns, and passive which he might allow. Pulling out the plugs on life-preserving machinery is "passive" (and therefore allowed). Administering increasingly heavy (and therefore life-shortening) doses of pain-killer is "active." Is this therefore to be condemned? The distinction seems more one of technique and type of ailment rather than of morality.

However you judge sacralistic rationalization of difficult cases, the basic thrust is clear. Human life in and of itself is a value commanding our moral respect beyond all considerations of convenience, technology and expediency. The focus is on life rather than on quality of life, though the latter at times enters into the calculus. Defective children are as valuable as are normal children. Foetal tissue demands a respect not accorded to other maternal tissue. The sick and elderly may not be done away with though their productive lives have ended. My life is a gift to be used wisely, but the time of my death is no more mine to decide than was the time of my birth. Still less is it mine to decide whether another should be allowed to be born, or whether I should actively cause another to die. Unlike the technological imperative, the sacralistic imperative trusts more in the life force itself than it does in human science. And over against the ecological imperative the sacralist views the fact of life as more precious than the quality of life.

CONCLUSION

To bring a complicated chapter back into focus, recall our twofold purpose. First we stated alternative approaches to the definitions of human life ranging from the utilitarian to the evolutionary to the sacral. We viewed the impact of these definitions on the stages of human life, especially their perspectives on human foetal life, human adult life, and human terminal life. The second part of the chapter examined the ethical consequences of these various philosophies of man. We outlined how each would handle the morality of human control over human life. In turn, we reviewed the kinds of moral reasoning implied by the technological imperative, the ecological imperative, and the sacralistic imperative regarding current problems of control such as genetic experimentation, abortion, drug use, suicide, and euthanasia. The intent was not to treat all these issues in the detail that they need and deserve. The intent rather was to help you ask yourself two questions: (1) "What does 'human life' mean for me?" (2) "What moral guidelines do I hold with regard to the use and control of my own human life and death, and that of others?"

As we hinted above, this narrow preoccupation with *human* life might be considered to be rather chauvinistic. Compared to the infinite cosmos and the universal life force, the survival of the human species or of any member of it could seem a puny matter indeed. However, that leads to yet another philosophy of man, and doubtless to another set of moral conclusions on the moral import of human life and death!

EIGHT:SOCIETY-LIFE TOGETHER

I hate war as only a soldier who has lived it can, only as one who has seen its brutality, its futility, its stupidity.

Dwight D. Eisenhower

Law is merely the expression of the will of the strongest for the time being, and therefore laws have no fixity, but shift from generation to generation.

Brooks Adams

Never do anything against your conscience, even if the state demands it.

Albert Einstein

I am liberating man from the degrading chimera known as conscience.

Adolf Hitler

The last chapter focused for the most part on personal moral decisions involving my own life and that of my relatives and unborn children. Decisions about euthanasia, abortion, and the use and abuse of drugs I feel are subject to my personal control. But does it make any sense to talk about morality in my public life? Can individual morality effectively extend beyond the sphere of family and personal acquaintances? What is the moral significance of the individual when pitted against the state? Does society at large, or even the society of mankind, raise any morally relevant issues for the individual? Must we be helpless moral pawns when national and even international pressures are brought to bear on us?

In simpler and happier times, the individual may have been able to excuse himself lightly from moral concern about affairs of state or society at large. What "they" did was beyond his care or control. The individual could be satisfied with being responsible and upright in his daily dealings, while leaving the larger issues to "them." But atrocities committed in the name of the state at time of war, corruption in government, abuse of the consumer by big business, and instantaneous communication have made it more impossible for the individual to morally wash his hands of these "larger" issues. And so we devote a chapter to some of the moral problems with which society at large confronts the individual.

The last chapter focused on the meaning of an individual human life. Now we are concerned with a philosophy of human society. How do and should individuals live together? We will consider the rule of war, the rule of law, and the rule of conscience. These rules governing human relationships are closely interconnected and often come into conflict. The crusty, early modern, British philosopher Thomas Hobbes felt that the basic principle governing human relations was hostility and war. So he argued for an absolutely powerful state as the only way to make society possible.[1] From a consideration of Hobbes we will move to a more optimistic philosophy which believes that men can live together under the rule of reasonable limited law. Finally we will consider the role of individual conscience in the face of law. In the course of developing these social philosophies, you will be challenged to take a stand regarding the morality of war, the moral obligation to obey the law, and the moral right of conscientious objectors against the law to be accorded amnesty. This chapter, then, is divided into the following three sections: (1) War: The State of Nature, (2) Law: The Nature of the State, and (3) Conscience: Individual and State.

WAR: THE STATE OF NATURE

As we will make clear below, your moral assessment of war will be a good barometer of what your philosophies of law and conscience are. The following little test will help you form a preliminary idea of where you stand.

Your War IQ

Which of the following three positions most closely expresses your moral evaluation of war?

Militarism. The question of war does not fit into ordinary ethical frameworks. It is the expression of an animal aggressive instinct in human beings which lies beneath and beyond rational control. It has its own morality, which is really *a-morality*. The law of the battlefield is survival, blind obedience, and sometimes glory. Ordinary norms don't apply. Violence in every animal species has a positive role to play in evolutionary survival and growth.

Just War Theory. Human life is not an absolute value. Some values are more precious than life itself, e.g., the preservation of a government which guarantees freedom, the maintaining of national boundaries in the face of attack, or the maintaining of economic advantage. When all other means fail, these are worth fighting and killing and dying for. Of course, there should be a proportion to the evils inflicted by war and the values I'm trying to preserve. Participation in war can sometimes be a morally good decision if it is based on the principle of choosing the lesser of two evils—choosing between fighting for my ideals or surrendering them.

Pacifism. Human life is an absolute value to be absolutely respected. Nothing can ever justify the systematic mass destruction of human life involved in the war system. And never can war be justified on the principle of the lesser of two evils. We are not reduced to the two evils of either mass murder or surrender of ideals. There is always a positive good alternative, viz., non-violent resistance and defense of ideals. This is not passivism, but pacifism. It is soul-power, *satyagraha*, a force. It is effective. The enemy will eventually stop killing those who resist but do not kill in return. He will come to sense our common humanity. And my forceful non-cooperation will make any enemy victory a hollow "victory" indeed.

With which of the following moral statements do you agree? Which of the three types of thinking described above does each statement represent? Place the number 1, 2, or 3 in the space provided after each statement. Which type of thinking determined your agreement or disagreement in each case?

    1. Lieutenant Calley should never have been indicted for war crimes.   _____

2. Conscientious objection to the Vietnam war was justified on the principle of the Nuremberg trials. _____

3. To conscientiously object to some wars and not to others is hypocrisy. _____

4. All attempts to justify war on ethical grounds are empty rationalizations. _____

5. Better red than dead. _____

6. Better dead than red. _____

7. Better non-violent resistance than red. _____

8. Complete amnesty is a *right* of exiled conscientious objectors, not a privilege for which they should beg. _____

9. War is a necessary evil. _____

10. War is a biological good. _____

11. Might makes right. _____

12. Right makes might. _____

13. To die as a loving but resisting martyr is superior to being killed in a contest of brutality. _____

14. In rejecting violence I have to be ready to accept the disappearance of all enforceable immigration quotas. _____

15. War and the threat of war is a necessary means for guarding America's corner on world resources that gives us our high living standard. Abolish the military system and our standard of living will radically drop as world wealth is redistributed.

_____

Legal Absolutism: Thomas Hobbes

A militaristic approach to war goes hand in hand with a "might makes right" philosophy of law. Individual conscience must take a back seat in this framework. Let's don the robes of the moral legalist and consider the philosophy of Thomas Hobbes.

For Hobbes and his modern counterparts, war is a biological human necessity. Civilization and law are a thin veneer covering the basic selfish animosity that every individual must adopt toward every other individual if he is to survive. To show the truth of this, Hobbes asks you to imagine what things would be like if there were no government, no army, no police, no prisons. In other words, imagine man living in what Hobbes calls "the state of nature" where there would be no laws or law enforcement. In such a state of affairs, says Hobbes, every man would be the equal of every other man. Why? Because even the weakest could inflict the supreme evil—death—

upon the strongest. Each man would be thrown back upon his own resources alone in order to survive in this world where the great leveler would be the power of each to inflict death on the other. This "state of nature," then, would be a state of "war of every man against every man," to use the words of Hobbes. There would be but one natural right—the right of every man to take all the means necessary for self-preservation.

Of course, this "state of nature" is a mental construct. But it does reveal man's basic essence, says Hobbes. It is no mere idle imagining. Consider your own everyday attitudes toward your fellow humans. Are you able to calmly walk the city streets alone at night? Do you own one of the tens of millions of hand guns privately possessed in America today? You lock and bolt the doors at night, when you go out. You have chests and cabinets locked in your own home and rent safety deposit boxes for what you dare not leave in your own home. Consider what happens in times of natural disaster. Homes and stores are looted. Even the jewelry on the bodies of the dead is not secure. A one-day police strike in Montreal recently triggered dozens of bank robberies. Civilized law and order is a thin veneer indeed.

Human beings, then, are basically individual atomic units, each locked in battle with the others, each struggling for his individual survival. This is intolerable. The "state of nature" is a state of fear. In it there could be no industry, no civilization, no arts, no social life, no leisure, no right or wrong, no justice or injustice beyond the right of every individual to preserve his own life at all costs. In Hobbe's words, "the life of man [would be] solitary, poor, nasty, brutish, and short." How is such a collection of antagonistic human atoms brought together into society?

An enlightened egoism draws certain conclusions from this intolerable "state of nature." These conclusions, called by Hobbes the "dictates of reason," impel man away from fear and insecurity toward happiness and security. First, each man should try for peace, though of course if that fails he has the right to fight for survival. Second, each man should be willing to give up his power over others to the extent that they give up theirs toward him, and be content with as much liberty regarding others as they have regarding him. Finally, each man should keep his contracts or agreements.

It is these dictates of enlightened egoism which lead men to the (implied) social contract by which the state is formed and society becomes possible. Reason alone is not enough to force men to live together. The countervailing passions are so strong that external force must be brought to bear. So I give up my power and my right of governing myself to the state, on condition that you do the same. The sovereign power now (in the form of king, dictator, democracy, or oligarchy) uses the strength and power of all for peace and common defense. Since the sovereign now is and has the supreme and only power, he (it) can terrify his antagonistic atomic subjects into living together in peace. The sovereign's will becomes absolute law, because the alternative is the intolerable chaos and fear of the "state of nature." The sovereign's *will* creates the state. And the state has the supreme power to physically enforce that will.

So man's natural state is to be at war. Society, Hobbes says, is an artificial creation. We give the sovereign supreme power in order that he (it) can force us to live together almost in spite of ourselves. This artificial body called the state is a precarious construct. If it breaks down, we are back to our natural condition where the law of the jungle obtains. This Hobbesian social philosophy leads to some pretty definite and inescapable conclusions regarding the philosophy of law, the philosophy of conscience, and the philosophy of war.

First, the law is to be obeyed simply and only because it is the *will* of the sovereign power. Remember, "sovereign" refers to any form of established government, i.e., a monarchy, a dictatorship or a constitutional republic like that of the United States. Once the sovereign will is made known and expressed in a law, that's it. The law is a *just* law not because the sovereign says "it is *reasonable*," but simply because the sovereign says "I *will* it." This legal philosophy is voluntaristic rather than rational. There is no higher law than the law of the land. There can be no appeal to a natural law, or a law of God, or even a law of reason, that could justify breaking the law of the land. Every law is a just law, simply because it is a law. An "unjust law" is a contradiction in terms.

You can compare this voluntaristic legal philosophy to certain religious moralities based on the "will of God." "God's will" determines what's good and what's bad. If God says, "Abraham, kill your son," then the killing is good because God said so. He so willed it. If God says, "Thou shalt not kill," then killing is bad, because God said so. It's not a question of whether killing is reasonable or good in itself. It's a question rather of what God's will happens to be that day. What he wills as good today, he can will as bad tomorrow. So it is with the sovereign rule of law in Hobbes' philosophy. If there is a law against smoking marijuana today, then it is immoral to break that law, and smoke. If there is a law tomorrow commanding everyone to smoke three joints a day, then it is immoral *not* to smoke. The question is not whether smoking pot is good or bad in itself, or whether it is reasonable, or whether it agrees with my religion. The only question is: What does the law say? The law is morality. Morality is the law. Man is morally free only where the law falls short, where the law is silent. Hobbes's morality is a morality of absolute legalism. I show moral responsibility not by deciding whether or not the law is reasonable and therefore to be obeyed. My single moral responsibility is to obey, period.

You ask Hobbes: "What about the sovereign? Is he above the law?" In a sense he is. He makes the law. He creates good and evil. There's no higher law to which he must submit. There is no external tribunal before which he could be summoned and tried. If there is any limit on him at all, it is in the internal forum of conscience, based on the dictates of reason. After all, the whole social contract is based upon the dictates of reason by which I am impelled to seek the kind of peace and self-preservation that is not available in the state of nature. The sovereign, then, cannot direct me to violate that basic instinct of self-preservation. He cannot rightly command what is inconsistent with the social contract. So he could not forbid me to defend myself against an attacker, or command that I testify against myself, or (interestingly enough) take away my right to pay a mercenary to take my place in the army in time of war! So the sway of the sovereign power is not absolutely unlimited. But we must hope that our governors follow these dictates of reason in their consciences, because there is no higher law or power which can force them to do so. They are the law. Their will creates both public and private morality.

As you'd expect, where the state is absolute, the role of individual conscience is at a minimum. All dissent is treason. Anyone who would urge that a law be broken because it violates some alleged "higher" law, is by that very fact a traitor. One often detects these Hobbesian accents in the speeches of high government officials, even in America. Those who dissent from established policies are branded as traitors. Loyalty is conformity. Conformity is the only alternative to utter chaos. Absolute obedience to law under the social contract is the only thing this side of the anarchy, the chaos, and the intolerable fear which exists in the state of nature. The dictates of reason impel us to seek security over freedom. There can be no chinks allowed in the legal armor that protects that security. The limited freedom that we do have is based on the absolute rule of law. There is no freedom in the jungle law of the "state of nature." It's law or anarchy—take your choice. Hobbes chooses law.

In this framework, there is no real problem regarding the morality of war. Every war legitimately engaged in between established governments is a just war. It is just, first of all, because the sovereign said so. He willed it. Second, wars are just and moral, because in relations between nations the "state of nature" is not a fiction or an imaginary construct. There is no world government. There is no supreme global power to terrify nations into living at peace with one another in the way that individual governments terrify their subjects into peaceful coexistence. Each nation, then, has the right to take all means necessary for self-preservation. And this often includes wars, defensive, preventative, and even expansive. If nuclear arms proliferate, we would quite literally be in the intolerable situation of Hobbes's "state of nature." The weakest nation would have the capability of destroying the strongest. If things ever come to such a pass, we might hope that the dictates of reason would impel us to form a global social contract where every nation surrenders its power to a supreme power, provided that every other nation does the same. And a global sovereign power could enforce a world peace that would be an alternative to the terrors of a nuclear state of nature.

Hobbes's philosophy of revolution is more interesting. In a state where dissent is treason, even the mildest forms of civil disobedience are out of the question. Dissent and civil disobedience, since they undermine the law, strike at the foundation of the state itself. In principle, they cannot fail to be construed as acts aimed at the overthrow of the government. It would follow, of course, that amnesty for war objectors is unthinkable. Rather they should be shot as traitors. There is, however, room for revolution in Hobbes's social philosophy— provided that it is a *successful* revolution!

The sovereign is to be obeyed only as long as he is effectively powerful enough to protect us. Whereas unsuccessful revolutionaries deserve to be shot, successful revolutionaries who form an effective new government can legitimately command obedience. That is why, if the American Revolution had failed, George Washington would have deserved to be executed as a traitor to the legitimate power vested in the British throne. But as things turned out, it was Benedict Arnold who met the traitor's punishment. Might makes right. The sovereign's will is law. For it is only through the power of an effective government that we are rescued from the terrors of the state of nature.

LAW: THE NATURE OF THE STATE

There is a more optimistic way to view man in society. Perhaps the rule of naked power need not be the only force that binds us together. Let us outline another view, where authority is based on law, and is not above the law but limited by it, and where law is based on reason and is not absolute, but is subject to the higher court of reason itself. Such a social philosophy will view the role of war, the role of law, and the role of conscience much differently than does Hobbes.

Limited Law: R.L. Cunningham

Let's start with the idea of authority. Why should one human being ever obey or submit to another human being? Hobbes's answer was quite forthright. You submit to authority because authority has physical clout. You submit only as long as and to the extent that authority can physically force you to submit. But this really doesn't do justice to the reason why men obey the law. We'd need a policeman for every citizen if this were actually the case. We obey the law because it is reasonable. It is basically to our best interest to do so. True, there is an instinct for individual survival. Hobbes went too far when he inferred that this instinct caused a state of war of every man against every other man. For we have an equally basic instinct to co-operate and live together. Even Hobbes's "dictates of reason" give dim recognition to this instinct. But this cooperative socializing side of man's nature deserves much more emphasis than it received from Hobbes. Law and authority are simply man's reasonable efforts to translate these socializing impulses into an actual livable society. It is in this framework that contemporary philosopher R.L. Cunningham has developed a philosophy of limited authority and law based on reason.[2] Let's see what Cunningham means by authority and then take a critical look at Hobbes through Cunningham's eyes.

"Authority," says Cunningham, "has two basically different meanings." Their confusion can easily lead to "crises of authority." First, an authority can mean an *expert*. Doctors, lawyers, scientists, and connoisseurs of wine are authorities in this sense. A physician could be *an* authority on diseases of the heart. A lawyer could be *an* authority on constitutional law. Cunningham calls such experts "an-authorities." Their function is to be carefully distinguished from that of another group called "in-authorities." It is the people involved in the in-authority game that chiefly concern us in this chapter.

Presidents, policemen, parents, like governors, gatekeepers, and game wardens all function in some degree as *in*-authorities. They are somehow "in charge." Where an-authorities give expert advice and testimony, these in-authorities give orders. "Halt!" says the gate- keeper. "Take out the garbage," the mother tells her son. "I declare the hurricane-devastated Carolina coast to be a disaster area," pro- claims the president. With regard to these two types of authority, let's see what the qualifications are for each, why anyone should pay at- tention to either type, and what the limits are to each of these two au- thority games. Note, that unlike the Hobbesian world of absolute au- thority, we are looking for *limits* on authority, without neglecting the basis of a moral obligation to respect it.

Obviously, the process of being put in charge over people is dif- ferent from the process of qualifying as an expert for people. Mayors get elected, parents beget children, and liquor commissioners get ap- pointed. However, election, procreation and appointment do not nec- essarily make these various in-authorities into experts (though one might hope that they have expertise). These, rather, are various ways in which they are put in charge of their respective kingdoms. A law- yer passes the bar exam, an orthodontist is accepted by the dental as- sociation, an astronomer is invited to address his peers. None of these events puts the various an-authorities in charge of anybody. These, rather, are various signs of their recognition as experts in their re- spective fields.

What response can authority rightly demand of me? When does it make moral sense for me to accept what another person says as a guide for my own behavior? It depends on which type of authority I am talking about. Briefly, an-authority can command my assent, but not my obedience. In-authority, on the other hand, can command my obedience even though I need not or cannot assent to the wisdom of his command. In other words, I can be *in* authority without necessari- ly being *an* authority on anything. And conversely, just because I'm *an* authority in a certain field doesn't put me *in* authority over any- one.

It's not hard to see why I should listen to experts. An-authorities are in the truth game. They have knowledge which I don't have. I pay to consult their expertise. It is rational and moral to assent, to believe what they say. When my doctor tells me that smoking is what causes my chronic cough, I believe him. But if he orders me to stop smok- ing, that order of itself imposes no obligation upon me to obey. It is not in the same category as a "no smoking" sign on a public bus. The doctor is a medical expert. That makes him smarter than I am, but it doesn't put him in charge over me. He rightly commands my assent, but not my obedience. An-authorities exceed their limits when they pretend that their expertise qualifies them to give orders. A psychiatrist can testify as to a defendant's sanity, but only a judge can dismiss the case. The prosecution rightly objects when the psychiatrist asserts that the case should be dismissed. The expert is as good as his evidence. I ignore him at the price of my own folly. It is up to him to persuade me of the truth of what he says.

The case of my moral obligation to respond to in-authorities is not so obvious. As we saw, they are not necessarily in the truth game. Though they may consult experts, they need not *be* experts. I don't obey them because they are wise. At times, I may be morally obliged to obey a stupid law or follow a dumb leader! Why? When is it reasonable, and therefore moral, to obey the commands of in-authority? Cunningham does not confront us with the stark Hobbesian dilemma of absolute obedience as the only alternative to absolute chaos. While most laws are just, some may be unjust, in Cunningham's more moderate view. There is a time to obey, and there may be a time not to obey. A law, however, does not become unjust simply because it is not the wisest of laws. There are times when it is reasonable to obey an unwise authority. A look at the function of in-authority will enable us to determine its power and its limits.

Society could not function without in-authority. Humans banding together in the pursuit of common goals (this being a definition of society) is the *raison d'être* of in-authority. You don't achieve common goals without cooperation. Sometimes that cooperation is spontaneously forthcoming, and sometimes it isn't. When it isn't, you need someone in charge, a traffic director, a law, to get people working together for the common goal. You could never get an apartment building erected without a hierarchy of construction supervisors and foremen in charge of the operation. You could never have safe driving without laws governing speed, one-way streets, keeping to the right, and policemen in charge of enforcing these laws. Apartment house construction and traffic safety are goals which demand in-authorities because the cooperation required would not otherwise be forthcoming.

Society has other common goals like the possibility of communication in a mutually understandable language (in America that would be English), or like the need of its citizens to keep warm outdoors in wintertime (i.e., by wearing warm clothes). But such cooperation happens spontaneously. No laws are required to make us speak English or dress warmly in the winter. A law about wearing overcoats when the temperature dips below freezing, or requiring that in certain buildings only English may be spoken, would be a superfluous and odious law. In-authority is reasonable and legitimate only when cooperation toward a common goal is both necessary and non-spontaneous. So we have laws about wearing seatbelts but not about wearing overcoats. Bilingual Quebec has language laws requiring the use of both French and English in government transactions, while Washington, D.C., remains linguistically unregulated. In-authority, then, is reasonable, and I am therefore morally obliged to obey it, when three conditions are fulfilled. First, as a member of a society I share in its common goal. Second, the achievement of that goal demands cooperation. And finally, that cooperation is not spontaneous. When these three conditions are fulfilled, in-authority is the mechanism that makes society work. It is this pragmatic function, then, i.e., "to make society work," that is the essence of in-authority. Of itself, it does not have a truth function. When in-authority confuses these two functions, it exceeds its limits; it's out of line. Did you ever have a boss, for example, who thought that just because he was the boss he knew it all? One hopes that the boss is smart, of course, but what he gets paid for is to make decisions. Without someone to make at least imperfect decisions, the business would come tumbling down. Without some, perhaps inferior, battle plan to capture an enemy emplacement, the attackers would be destroyed. And you can't put a bunch of carpenters, electricians, masons, and plumbers on an empty lot and just tell them to "go to it." The boss, the general, and the foremen are needed to orchestrate a concerted action.

But such decisions-makers, necessary though they be, are not automatically endowed with expertise. When a general starts acting like an expert on international politics, he's rightly fired, just as you'd rightly ignore your boss's assumption of expertise about how you should vote or raise your children. And you needn't even believe that his business decisions are right, though you may be morally obliged to obey them while you are in his employ. Poor decisions are better than no decisions at all. For example, if a law were passed that as of tomorrow all automobiles on U.S. roads should keep to the left, it would be reasonable and moral (and healthy!) to obey such a law, however stupid that law might be. I obey in-authorities because under certain conditions (i.e., *a common goal requiring necessary and nonspontaneous cooperation*) the alternative of non-compliance with in-authority is worse.

So Cunningham proposes a limited and rational philosophy of law and authority compared to the absolute and voluntaristic philosophy of Hobbes. Let's return now to the questions of war and amnesty as viewed in this more limited framework. Clearly in this view, no authority, no war, no law is just and moral simply on the sovereign's say-so. The citizen has the duty to obey, when in-authority is exercised within its reasonable limits, and the right to conscientiously disobey when in-authority exceeds its legitimate limits. By what criteria does a citizen judge his government's laws? Let's say right off that he may not conscientiously disregard a law simply because he thinks it's an unwise law or a poor one, or one upon which he could improve. No, a law is just and moral provided that it comes within the purview of in-authority's pragmatic function, namely, to ensure the necessary and non-spontaneous cooperation of citizens toward their country's common goals. Any law that meets these conditions, I must obey. Where a law fails this test, there is room for conscientious objection.

It is on grounds such as these that many exiled objectors against America's Vietnam escapade demand amnesty and repatriation as moral rights. They judged that *this* war and *this* military conscription law exceeded the limits of in-authority. These are the "selective objectors." Unlike absolute pacifists, these relative pacifists are not morally opposed to *all* war. Unlike Hobbesian citizens, they do not automatically submit to all laws. They pick and choose their wars; they pick and choose their laws. This middle position infuriates both absolute authoritarians and absolute pacifists alike. What right do these people have to pick and choose which wars they will fight and which laws they will obey? If this "picking and choosing" were based upon arbitrary subjective whim, it would indeed be morally indefensible. But Cunningham gives a rational basis for judging the justice or injustice of a particular law or of a particular war. In-authority is neither to be blindly followed nor arbitrarily rejected. Rather it is to be judged in the court of reason. And reason asks three questions of in-authority's command. First: Is this law consistent with the common goal of the society to which I belong? Second: Is the cooperation which is demanded of me really a necessary means toward achieving this goal? (I would presume that the cooperation demanded is not a manifest evil in itself—e.g., a command to consign fellow citizens to gas chambers. Cunningham does not subscribe to the doctrine that the end justifies the means.) And finally, is this cooperation unlikely to occur spontaneously? Cunningham's citizen can rightly put such questions to the sovereign and either obey or morally disobey according to the arrived-at answers.

Let us grant right off that the answers to such questions are seldom clear, and grant, further, that the presumption be on the side of the law. Still, the point we make here, following Cunningham, is that there *is* room for individual conscience in the face of the law. An individual need not surrender the direction of his conscience to the state. Morality is not identical with law, but is the judge of law. There can be moral laws and immoral laws, just wars and unjust wars, and the individual may not morally abdicate his responsibility of deciding between them as far as he is able.

Volumes have been written during the past decade on the function of war, the inevitability of aggression, and the need for defensive violence in human affairs. Philosophers, anthropologists, historians, psychologists and theologians have each had their say. Wars go on and lives are destroyed with brutalized mass efficiency even as citizens develop a numbed protective insensibility to the relentless barrage of the claims, counterclaims and daily atrocities reported in the media. Those who are able to remain sensitive to the human reality of such events find themselves impelled to take a conscientious stand. The major philosophical options regarding the morality of war were outlined in the beginning section of this chapter: "Your War IQ." We will not further develop these options here. War is a trillion dollar industry, global in scope, and far out of any individual's power to control. So rather than developing (beyond the mere outline) a moral evaluation of war as an objective reality with its own overwhelming momentum, we have focused on the role of individual conscience *vis-à-vis* war, and more precisely, *vis-à-vis* the state which wages war. In the Hobbesian view, the state's absolute power must all but quench conscience's individual light. Cunningham shows how that flame of conscience may burn brightly and steadily with loyalty untainted as it strives to purify the excesses of in-authority. We will now outline a third view which makes conscience all supreme.

CONSCIENCE: INDIVIDUAL AND STATE

Recalling Kohlberg's descriptive analysis of the stages of moral growth (see Chapter Two), we could view Hobbes's philosophy as a classic expression of that fourth "law and order" stage of moral decision-making. Cunningham's philosophy of law is in line with Kohlberg's stage five morality, where reason rather than law is in the moral driver's seat. The law is respected, but the human thinking community is greater than any sovereign's law. Human reason will insist upon the right of distinguishing between just and unjust laws (and wars), and of acting accordingly. Kohlberg's stage six is the pinnacle of moral maturity, the "universal ethical principle" orientation.

Here dwells the moral absolutist in the sense of the totally autonomous decision-maker. He is the idealist, the prophet, the man who has thought his values through and will put himself on the line for them whatever be the cost. He dares to stand alone if need be. There are no shortcuts to such maturity. It is not arrived at cheaply. The lower stages must be lived through and transcended.

Of course, a man's moral response to his country's call to arms can be positive or negative. You can deduce nothing about his moral maturity from *what* decision he makes about war. Absolute pacifists (i.e., those who reject *all* war) do not by that fact alone rate accolades for moral superiority. Six men could adopt the moral stance of absolute pacifism for motivations that range from the infantile to the adult. I could reject all war (1) because of automatic guilt feelings that anyone who uses a gun will go to hell, or (2) because the risk and pain of military life are too unpleasant, or (3) because all my best friends are conscientious objectors and expect me to be too, or (4) because my religion forbids war, or (5) because I have rationally concluded that this war is unjust and doing my country more harm than good, or (6) because I have come to respect human life so absolutely that I could never harm it in any way, least of all by participating in the system of mass killing called war.

Absolute Pacifism: Gandhi

For the completely autonomous moral adult of stage six, conscience reigns supreme. However, he wasn't born that way. In him like everyone else, a superego first was formed which internalized parental moral taboos. Then he had to learn to weigh the feedback of pleasurable and painful consequences resulting from his various decisions. As he grew, he came to value other people whose approval he needed even at the cost of his selfish desires. He then develops further, cutting the approval-disapproval umbilical cord in the name of a higher duty and law. And if he matures to a post-conventional morality, he has to transcend even the law, with the realization that there can be conflicting laws and that all laws are not just. Finally, he becomes morally his own man with his own values, fearing self-condemnation more than the condemnation or disapproval of rational men.

Such a liberated human being in whom conscience is supreme, has what Gandhi called *satyagraha*, "soul-force." He knows from experience what reward and punishment are, what approval and disapproval mean, and he has learned duty and respect for law. In the harsh moral school of actual decision-making, he has learned to stand alone if need be. Such a philosophy of the absolute supremacy of conscience in the face of law is not abstract. It's not something you read in a book and then apply to life. Gandhi, the absolute pacifist, the extoller of *satyagraha*, said that if he had a choice between a coward or a militarist, he'd pick the latter every time. Non-violent force (*satyagraha*) for one's ideals can be practiced only by those who are ready to die. Those who have achieved such liberation from a fear of death can rejoice in a conscience which is not opposed to the law or above the law, but rather is beyond the law. It is in this spirit that they would resist a country's call to arms. It would not be the *passivism* of doormats, but a *pacifism* which acts, though non-violently, against the taking of human life. It is in this spirit that they would actively refuse to cooperate with laws that they believed to be unjust. While others, less mature, might rally under the banner of absolute pacifism, these alone have earned the right to do it in the name of consciences truly liberated. I personally would say that these, above all, deserve their country's amnesty of such conscientious disobedience, perhaps because their moral decisions were most detached and liberated from thoughts of amnesty to begin with.

CONCLUSION

We have reviewed three basic philosophies of how men live together in society. Consider again the questions at the beginning of the chapter. Are men hostile atomic units who need to be physically forced to live together under the absolute rule of law? Or do there exist instincts of cooperation and reason which bring us together under the gentle nudging of a limited "in-authority"? Or finally, can we work for a moral utopia where through an unswerving commitment to conscience in love men can live together in peace beyond all consideration of law? Each of these social philosophies, we saw, will view in a different light the role of conscience, the role of the state, and the role of law. Their differing premises will yield different norms for arbitrating conflicts between individual and state, conscience and law, and the moral possibilities of war and peace. These tensions doubtless will be always with us. But fortunately it is rare that I must face such nakedly dramatic confrontations in my day to day decisions. It is the interactions of man and man rather than the confrontations of individual and state that take up the bulk of my moral life.

Justice and equality rather than revolution and civil disobedience are what preoccupy us. Witness our headlines: unions and strikes, power struggles and liberation movements. These form the substance of *justice* which is one of today's most urgent moral concerns. "Justice: Who Needs It?" That's the title and subject of the chapter now following.

NINE: JUSTICE: WHO NEEDS IT?

Extreme justice is extreme injustice.

Marcus Tullius Cicero

Justice is truth in action.

Benjamin Disraeli

*One of the greatest disasters that happened to modern civiliza-
tion was for democracy to inscribe "liberty" on its banners instead of "justice." Because "liberty" was considered the ideal it
was not long until some men interpreted it as meaning "freedom
from justice." The industrial and social injustice of our era is the
tragic aftermath of democracy's overemphasis on freedom as the
"right to do whatever you please." No, freedom means the right
to do what you* ought, *and* ought *implies law, and law implies
justice.*

Fulton J. Sheen

There is no corner of the earth that does not resound with the cry
for justice. The "Third World" is stirring like a sleeping giant. Men
no longer will quietly consent to being treated like second class
humans (nor will women!). The call is for equality. And this equality
is the basis of justice. Justice means rights and the duty to respect

145

these rights. Women's rights, black rights, Indian rights, property rights, opportunity rights and welfare rights all vie for recognition in the national and world arenas. Exploration of the issues raised by these movements to obtain justice could fill volumes.

In this chapter we will focus on an issue most vexing to our contemporary American society, the problem of reverse discrimination as a method of remedying past and present injustice. We will examine the morality of reverse discrimination as it touches on female and black "minorities." It is hoped that the principles developed in this discussion can be extended by the reader to other areas of social concern.

Before going any further, give yourself a little test of where your mind and heart are in matters of justice. The questions range beyond the areas to be treated in this chapter, but they will give you a feel for the kind of issues involved in a discussion of moral justice.

Your Justice IQ

How would you rank in order of importance the following three principles as governing just relations among men?

Equalitarian Justice: All men are equal, as free and self-aware human beings; therefore no human being should be used as a means or an instrument for any other human being.

Meritarian Justice: All men are not equal; they differ in talent, productivity and merit; equality of treatment should be based on merit, e.g., as far as possible, equal pay for equal work, and equal opportunity for equal talent.

Welfare Justice: All men have basic human needs of food, shelter, education, and medical care; each, therefore, is entitled to have these basic needs filled, regardless of his merits.

*Read the following moral statements about justice. Put a +
beside those you agree with and an X beside those statements with
which you disagree.*

The state should provide free child day care so that any woman who wants to may have the opportunity to work.   ____

As a home owner, I have the right to sell or not to sell it to anyone I please.   ____

Every American has the right to a college education.   ____

Private clubs have the absolute right to establish their own membership rules.   ____

Equal education is the right of every child, even if it means busing to obtain racial and educational balance in the schools.   ____

A woman as much as a man has the right to control her own body; therefore, the state should provide for free abortion for all who request it and cannot afford to pay.   ____

Any person, regardless of his race, has a right to buy a home in any neighborhood he can afford.   ____

The airlines should give the same job opportunities to male cabin attendants and fat stewardesses that they accord to slim female ones.   ____

The disproportionate share of the world's wealth controlled by Americans is objectively immoral and unjust.   ____

Private schools have the perfect right to exclude all applicants who do not pass the entrance tests or who are unable to pay.   ____

A poor man has no right to money and services which he has not earned.   ____

Law and medical schools should admit minority group applicants (e.g., blacks, Puerto Ricans, and women) in preference to other equally or better qualified applicants in order to redress the present under-representation of these groups in the legal and medical professions.   ____

As a car owner, I have a right to sell or not to sell it to anyone I please.   ____

No one should be refused membership in a club on the basis of sex.   ____

The structure of society (national and international) remains basically unjust until every human being has a guaranteed annual income for his basic human needs.   ____

Now go back over the fifteen moral statements once again. Ask yourself which type of justice governed your decision in each case. In the space provided after each statement note whether it was equalitarian justice (EJ), meritarian justice (MJ), or welfare justice (WJ).

That's the end of the test. Let's look at your answers. Your politics reflects your moral orientation. Were merit, talent, and productivity your prevailing norms? If so, your answers are in the best tradition of *laissez-faire* capitalism. Your philosophy is in the camp of Ayn Rand's objectivism (see Chapter Six). And your morality is individualistic, even anti-social, as we will see. Was welfare uppermost in your mind, i.e., the redistribution of wealth and the right of every person to have his human needs satisfied? Then your political ideal is communistic (this doesn't mean totalitarian). Your philosophy might have a Marxist orientation. And in morality you truly believe that no man is an island and that we are our brothers' keepers. Or finally, was equalitarian justice your main concern? If so, your politics are less dogmatic. Your philosophy doubtless is an effort to balance over against each other private merit and public good. And your morality will try to make a place for individual differences which nevertheless respect the basic equality of human beings.

The conflicting demands of justice and the precarious tension between individual merit and common welfare come to a dramatic head in the contemporary problem of reverse discrimination on the basis of race or sex. Discrimination on grounds of justice—what a paradox! Justice says "equal." Discrimination says "unequal." Isn't the very idea of a *just discrimination* a contradiction in terms? This problem will be the first consideration of this chapter. Then the second part of the chapter will explicitly apply our conclusions to contemporary sexist and racist movements for justice.

DOES DISCRIMINATION MEAN INJUSTICE?

"Discrimination" has become a bad word. It was not always thus. In fact, it is still a compliment to call someone a "discriminating" person. "Discriminating," according to the *American Heritage Dictionary*, means "perceptive," "able to draw fine distinctions." A discriminating connoisseur could distinguish good wine from bad. A discriminating football scout could distinguish promising young players from the run-of-the-mill variety. A discriminating editor can distinguish manuscripts that will sell from those that will flop. The word discriminating, then, is often used to mean the ability to distinguish good from bad. The discriminating man distinguishes in favor of one item and against another. So discrimination takes on the character of making a value judgment.

Equality Versus Merit

To discriminate in the area of sex seems to mean not merely to distinguish men from women, but to discriminate in favor of men as against women (or the other way around). In the matter of race, to distinguish black from white seems to mean not merely that black and white are different, but that black is superior to white (or the other way around). Discrimination, then, which originally meant a neutral recognition of differences, now comes to imply a negative value judgment, a discrimination *against*. Discrimination against poor wine is harmless enough. But when you are talking about human beings, isn't it unjust and immoral to discriminate against your fellow man? The answer is no, at least not always. Let's see now how we can distinguish discrimination which is just and moral from that which is not. And having sorted that out, we'll proceed to the question of reverse discrimination in the present. But first let's see if discrimination of any kind is ever moral.

Remember that discrimination can be a neutral word. In this sense, human society is unimaginable without it. Discrimination rests upon two incontrovertible facts: (1) all men are not equal; (2) men are different from one another. Discrimination is a recognition of these inequalities and differences so that one's conduct may be guided accordingly. This is called *meritarian justice*.

On the other hand, it is true to say that "all men are equal" and that "men are not different—they share a common humanity." To discriminate among human beings as if some were superhuman, some human, and some subhuman is unintelligent, unrealistic and therefore immoral. Refusal to discriminate here is a recognition of the common humanity that one shares with others so that one's conduct may be guided accordingly. This is called *equalitarian justice*.

Failure to discriminate, then, where discrimination is due is injustice. To take an absurd example, you wouldn't hire a kleptomaniac as a store detective in preference to a retired police officer in good standing. Here, discrimination is clearly just. It recognizes merit and talent and rewards it accordingly. And conversely, discrimination can also be unjust. Take the not unknown case of a woman who is refused entrance to medical school in favor of a less qualified male applicant. To discriminate thus on the basis of sex is to treat her as a second class human. This is a violation of equalitarian justice.

Therefore, discrimination is sometimes just and sometimes unjust; it's not always easy to decide. For example:

(1) Poverty discriminates, placing the poor in a class apart; welfare regulations are an attempt to discriminate between the deserving and the undeserving poor; guaranteed annual income is a proposal which refuses to discriminate among the poor. Here, which is just and which unjust—discrimination or refusal to discriminate?

(2) College entrance exams are an attempt to discriminate between qualified and unqualified applicants; open college admissions is

a policy which refuses to discriminate on the basis of merit or talent. Here, which is just and which is unjust—discrimination or refusal to discriminate?

(3) Work rules in a factory forbidding women to lift heavy weights discriminate protective working conditions for the "weaker sex"; a policy subjecting women to the same conditions as men is a refusal to discriminate on the basis of sex. Here, which is just and which is unjust—discrimination or refusal to discriminate?

Note, too, that even the non-discrimination proposals just mentioned involve discriminations on other levels. Guaranteed annual income does discriminate between the rich and the poor. Open college admissions do discriminate between those who have high school diplomas and those who don't. Equal working conditions for women do not extend to rest room facilities shared with males. How do I discern just discrimination from unjust?

Discrimination Is Sometimes Just

The case for discrimination in the area of poverty and race relations, for example, need not rest upon any intention of degrading the poor or of relegating minority groups to subhuman status. While respecting them as fellow human beings, the discriminator at the same time wants to face unsentimentally the realistic fact of differences and inequalities among men. I would like to have a summer home on the seashore, says the discriminator, but my salary is not large enough. You don't find me complaining that I should have one handed to me on a silver platter. It's a fact of life that some men have more money than others. This is a difference with which we have to live. We make economic discriminations in every area of life. There are some men to whom you are willing to risk lending money—others not. This is economic discrimination of a very intelligent and necessary kind. Therefore, when the poor want money handed out to them I'm not being inhuman when I say no. I'd like money handed out to me too, but I don't demand this as a right, because I recognize the fact that men are different in what they own and what they can earn, and money doesn't grow on trees. Discrimination between the rich and the poor is just and necessary. Anything else is naive sentimentality.

Not only is economic discrimination a necessary fact of life, unpalatable though it might be for people like myself who would like to have more money, says the discriminator, but discrimination on the basis of sex is perfectly reasonable and moral. Women are, after all, different from men, and *vive la différence*. To deny this on the alleged grounds of sexual equality is a violation of justice. It is a refusal to respect the peculiar genius, strength and weakness of each sex. So men get drafted into the army, not women. The "men's room" is not an exact replica of the "lady's room." Maternal leave for pregnant women is written into labor contracts. All of these discriminations are just and moral recognitions of real sexual differences. No movement can liberate women (or men, for that matter) from their biology.

Not only are human beings unequal in wealth and different in sex, but they differ in talent, training and merit. And these differences too should be recognized in justice. The more qualified student is the one who deserves to be admitted to medical school. The better trained applicant is the one who should get the job. So-called "reverse discrimination," says the discriminator, is a perverse denial of merit and is therefore unjust. The quota system is a racist sexist doctrine. A white male is not degrading blacks or women if he gets a job because he is more qualified than they are. He earned it. If they're better qualified, they've earned it.

Discrimination Is Sometimes Unjust

The case against discrimination in the treatment of minorities does not necessarily rest on the naive refusal to recognize the inequalities and differences among human beings, any more than the case for discrimination need imply that those discriminated against are inhuman. It is granted that persons are economically unequal. Every man does not have the inborn right to own a yacht. The demand for equality does not imply urinals in the "ladies room" or napkin dispensers in the "men's room." It is granted that humans differ in academic potential. It makes no sense for a grammar school dropout to demand admission to college.

These discriminations are just precisely because they do not discriminate against me as a human being. The fact that I am too poor to own a yacht does not make me less than human. Recognition that a woman's biology functions differently from a man's does not imply that she's less than the equal of a man. And saving the grammar school dropout from the bewilderment of a college classroom is not a judgment on his human dignity.

Discrimination gets to be unjust when it implicitly divides people up into superior human species and inferior human species, when it starts to imply not only that "female is different," but also that "female is inferior"; not only that "black is different," but that "black is inferior"; not only that "poor is different," but that "poor deserves a level of living that is below the human." When females, blacks, and the poor are treated as if they were not quite as human as males, whites, and the wealthy, then the discrimination becomes unjust. What may at first sight look like discrimination based on merit may turn out to be basically a discrimination that accords human dignity to some and not to others.

At long last we have arrived at the acid test for just and unjust discrimination. Am I being discriminated against precisely as a human being? Am I being treated as if I were less than human? This violates equalitarian justice. Animals like beef steer and turkeys may morally be used for man's own ends. However, a fellow human being, as equal and not inferior, should never be used as a mere means. On the other hand, does the discrimination apply to me not as human, but as a particular *kind* of human? This is perfectly just, provided that I am being treated with dignity and respect as a human.

It would, then, be a violation of human dignity to let a poor man starve to death because he couldn't afford food. But his human dignity could well survive his inability to afford a condominium for vacations in Key Biscayne. It may well be a violation of a woman's human dignity to refuse day care for her children so that she may have an opportunity to work that is equal to a man's opportunity. But her human dignity can well survive restriction to a bath house separate from males at public beaches. It would violate a black's human dignity to prefer a less qualified job candidate over him on the grounds of race alone. However, a white's human dignity might well survive his being excluded from the Afro-American Society on the grounds of race alone.

Adequate food, free child day care, and equal job opportunity are claimed by their advocates as rights, not privileges. Poor people, women, and blacks feel that they are being treated as something less than human when these rights are not honored. You may well object that free child day care, a balanced diet, and a college education are *not* necessarily connected with being human. And it is perfectly true that in a Polynesian society, for example, there are women, blacks, and poor people who are living contented, free and respected human lives without a college education, or child day care, or a balanced diet. And we need not recur to Polynesia. Here in the United States a generation or two ago college education was felt to be a privilege, not a right. The lack of higher education was not equivalent to closing a person off from the mainstream of American life. In the very recent past before the rise of liberated female consciousness, a woman felt (or felt she should feel) fulfillment and self-worth in a housewife's role. She readily ceded to her husband the breadwinner's task. Today higher education qualifies her to enter the formerly male preserve, and the pill makes her sexual life as liberated as the male's. These academic and biological changes have revolutionized the terms upon which a woman today can feel herself to be an equal and accepted member of American life. To exclude this new woman from the job market is to treat her as less than human. Discrimination can no longer rest (as it formerly might have) on her academic and biological disqualifications. Discrimination in these new circumstances would rest on the grounds of her sex alone. Discrimination would be another way of saying that there is a sexual caste system, and hers is the lower caste—a clear violation of equalitarian justice.

A person's dignity, hope, and chances for self-realization are a function of his ability to participate in, and be accepted by, the society in which he lives and finds his identity. The conditions for hope-filled human development in America 1975 are different from conditions for hope-filled human development in America 1935 (or even 1965). I can live with hope if my society accepts me, needs me, and lets me share in its work and growth and play. To the deadened poor in America today society says: "I don't need your help; I don't want to live with you; you are a burden to me; I wish you would go away." This is the human significance of adequate welfare legislation and open admissions to college. To disqualify a person from college in American society can mean to disqualify him as a human being. Similarly, to disqualify women from jobs or professions in American society can mean refusal to recognize them as full-fledged humans. To treat the poor, the black, and the female minorities as *different*, is one thing. Human differences demand recognition. But to treat them as *subhuman* is something else again. Human dignity they already possess: it is not a quality any person should have to earn.

REVERSE DISCRIMINATION

Equal human treatment, then, and reward for merit—these are ideals of justice with which few would quarrel. But there is another policy abroad today, proposed in the name of justice, but considered by many to be the depth of injustice. I'm talking now about reverse

discrimination. On the basis of race alone, blacks have been discriminated *against* in the past in educational and job opportunities. This
justifies today discrimination *in favor* of blacks on the basis of race,
so the argument goes, to remedy past injustice. On the basis of sex
alone, women have been *excluded* from certain careers in the past.
This justifies today the *inclusion* of women in these careers on the
basis of sex alone, even to the exclusion of equally or better qualified
males. Unjust past discrimination is to be remedied by present day
reverse discrimination.

This may seem just to formerly victimized minorities. But it
seems unjust indeed to the newly discriminated against victims. Discrimination in favor of blacks, the objection goes, is clearly discrimination against whites. It is immoral racism in a new guise. Only the
names of the victims have been changed. Discrimination in favor of
females is clearly discrimination against males. Carried to a logical
extreme, if women are to be equally represented on today's job market, this means either firing half the presently employed males, or else
excluding a generation of male job applicants until the female quota
is attained. Nothing so radical is seriously proposed. But the principle
is clear. Discrimination in favor of females can be achieved only at
the cost of male opportunities. It is sexism in a new guise. Only now
the male replaces the female as victim. So on the face of it, reverse
discrimination seems not to be justice, but a mockery of justice.

Basically, reverse discrimination rankles the white and the male
precisely because it does not recognize and reward their merit. It assumes that merit alone is not everything. I personally would propose
equalitarianism as the most basic ideal of human society. In this
view, a strict meritocracy would be inhuman and immoral. Let's look
at the philosophy of man underlying these assumptions which claim
to justify a policy of reverse discrimination.

Equalitarian philosophy clearly views all humans as belonging to
one species. There is no subgroup, or class, or caste of humans that is
inferior to or to be subordinated to another. Human dignity is something which every person already possesses. Respect for this dignity
need not be earned or merited. It is morally demanded by the mere
fact of one's membership in the human race. This philosophy rejects,
for example, a sexual caste system in which the female is inferior to
the male, and hence subordinate to him and owing him obedience, or
weaker than he and demanding his often patronizing "protection."
This philosophy rejects a racial caste system in which essentially inferior races are to be dominated by master races. A person might have
to *qualify* to be an astronaut, a pro quarterback, or a public school

teacher, but no one has to qualify to be a human being equal, as human, to any other human being. There is no specification sheet for membership in the human race besides being conceived and born. This all may seem obvious enough, but it has radical implications for the application of meritarian justice.

There are times, it is claimed, when *merit* is used to determine the qualifications for being treated as *human*. And the lack of certain merits equivalently relegates certain classes of people to a subhuman status in society. In other words, sometimes the rigid application of meritarian justice equivalently violates equalitarian justice. This is the key argument of the reverse discriminator. Treatment on the basis of merit alone sometimes means treatment of certain persons as less than human. In these cases, considerations of merit must give way to considerations of equality. This is what reverse discrimination sets out to do. It refuses to let considerations of merit alone disenfranchise certain classes of people from the human race.

It is precisely this disenfranchised status that has been laid upon women, blacks and other minorities. Or say, rather, that these groups had never been enfranchised to begin with. One remedy is "reverse discrimination." But this phrase has misleading connotations. It seems to imply that if the *original* discrimination was unjust, then it is legitimate to turn the tables on the original perpetrators and do an injustice to *them* via *reverse* discrimination! Reverse discrimination as understood by its advocates is not against anybody. Its whole focus is positive—to bring about a society that treats in a human way those groups which are now being treated as somehow subhuman. Phrases like compensatory discrimination and preferential hiring better express this positive goal. These policies are directed toward a society in which no one, whites and males included, will be used as the subhuman tool of an allegedly superior caste, and in which every person will have equal access to participation in the society in which he lives and enjoy the fruits of that participation.

This ideal state of affairs does not exist for women and blacks in America today. Law schools, for example, may not have intended in the past to keep blacks out of the legal profession. But the criteria for admission have just as effectively produced that very result. Less than one percent of American lawyers are black out of a black population of twelve percent. And what's the last time you saw a lady physician in the country where women outnumber men in the general population?

This is not simply a question of a numbers game. If that alone were the issue we'd be hearing a louder clamor than we do urging, for example, equal representation of women in the ranks of professional baseball. What's at issue are social needs as well as proportionate representation and individual justice. Without indicting all male psychiatrists and gynecologists, women have been complaining more and more about the patronizing and unsympathetic treatment accorded them by male physicians in these areas of particularly female sensitivity. There have indeed been increasing claims of out and out abuse. (We may note in passing that similar charges have been leveled at churches which have a predominately male clergy. The experience of many women is that these clergy, consciously or not, have effectively used religion to confine and maintain females in a subordinate sexual and religious caste. But that's another story.)

Moving to the legal profession which is entrusted with the delicate task of mediating conflicting public interests in the American melting pot, let's hear from the American Bar Association:

"Training lawyers for the work of accommodating and ordering conflicting interests of a pluralistic society requires a diverse and heterogeneous student body; a segregated law school will not afford an adequate education for a multi-racial practice."[1]

I would conclude, then, that, as in the medical profession so, too, here in the legal, both concrete considerations of social need and abstract considerations of equalitarian justice urge a redress of current injustices by some policy of preferential treatment of minorities.

This idea of preferential treatment is not some wild recent invention by blacks or by women's liberation. The favored treatment accorded by schools to the children of generous alumni, or by politicians to generous corporations is not unheard of in American society. Such long practiced exceptions to a rigid meritocracy have often operated against justice and the common good. The preferential policies that we have been discussing are based upon justice and the common good. They are unusual only in that they favor the oppressed minorities rather than the established holders of power. Accordingly, it is from this latter quarter that the shouts of anguish are the loudest.

Reverse discrimination, however, is no panacea. It's not without its problems: (1) How far should this principle be extended? (2) Will the results be truly effective? (3) Is it fair to the newly discriminated against victims?

To the first problem. Not *all* blacks, Puerto Ricans, and Chicanos (and certainly not all women) are "disadvantaged." Nor are all whites "advantaged!" And is reverse discrimination to be practiced in favor of other ethnic groups that are in some degree hindered by discrimination, i.e., Jews, Poles, Italians, Hungarians, Arabs?

When merit gives way to quotas, an epidemic can be unleashed.

Second, maybe what minorities need most of all is not lawyers and doctors of their own kind, but lawyers and doctors who are optimally qualified. Of course, sex might enhance a woman doctor's effectiveness with women patients as also race might enhance a black judge's ability to make judicious decisions for the black community. There is no assurance, however, that minority professionals will hasten to serve their own "constituencies." And finally, we might note that a double standard of admission to professional schools can easily lead to a double standard of grading or evaluation and the consequent stigma that minority professionals are not as well qualified as their "majority" colleagues.

Third, as we have noted before, discrimination in favor of minorities almost always involves discrimination against "majorities"—against qualified white males to cite the case in point. The community is asking the white male to pay the price of its past inhumanity. Advocates of reverse discrimination should face this cost squarely. True, meritarian justice may not be the absolute norm for all human relationships. It may occasionally have to give way to equalitarian justice. But the fact remains that meritarian justice *is* justice. *Quid pro quo*, equal pay for equal services, equal reward for equal merit, equal opportunity for equal qualifications—these demands of justice do not disappear even in a society which is trying to compensate for past wrongs. As a matter of fact women, blacks, and other minorities are striving to bring about a climate in which precisely their own *merits* will be recognized and rewarded. To do away altogether with the principle of merit is to defeat the ultimate good at which reverse discrimination is aiming. The temporary and selective suspension of the merit system in the case of qualified white males remains an evil to be tolerated, not a good in itself. Though it is an evil, it may be in present day America the lesser of two evils. The greater evil would be the continued relegating of minorities to a subhuman caste system.

A balance must be struck in the solution of the above conflicts arising out of a policy of reverse discrimination. On the one hand, a doctrinaire meritocracy would put some groups in a master race or master sex, dominating and using their "inferiors" to their own ends. No longer would there be one human race, all of whose members receive equal treatment as humans. A doctrinaire equalitarianism, on the other hand, ignores merit and talent and reduces all human beings to a least common denominator where uniqueness, freedom and talent count for next to nothing. In political terms, both *laissez-faire* capitalism ("merit is everything") and uncompromising communism ignore a dimension of human reality which is present and will not go away. Men are equal. But they are unique and different from each other too. Justice is the virtue which guides the relations of persons among themselves, and these two dimensions must be observed in any balanced philosophy of man.

As a closing note in the discussion of reverse discrimination, let's raise a more profound issue that would require several volumes on its own.[2] I suggest that the basic problem of injustice in America is not racial or sexual or ethnical discrimination. The problem goes much deeper, and racial and sexual inequalities are simply conspicuous surface symptoms of it. American society, maybe more than most others, has an unequally skewed reward system which results in great disparities of wealth. This consequently divides Americans into the top group of superhumans who are most admired, the middle group of average humans, and the poor who hardly count as human at all. Money is the main determiner of which group you belong to and of how humanly or subhumanly you'll be treated. In India the *sanyassin* who wanders about half naked begging for his bread is an object of respect and admiration. But such a character wandering about on American streets would be charged with vagrancy and thrown into jail. Granting the religious and cultural problems with this little illustration, the point remains that in America money is the main source of the social esteem one receives as a human being and consequently of one's own self-esteem as a human being.

Next question: Who gets the money? In the capitalistic West, the answer to this question is that economic reward is a function of demand. Which humans are in greatest demand? Look at the salaries and benefits: professional athletes, top executives, doctors, talented singers, etc. In a word, the intelligent, the graceful, and the "beautiful" people are in demand. They are the ones who are rewarded. They count even as superhuman if they are supersuccesses. The ugly, the defective and the stupid are lucky to get enough to eat and stay out of the cold. That is to say, they are lucky to receive any minimum human treatment at all. You are human in America to the extent that you are productive and marketable. Membership in the human race indeed does have to be earned in America. This is the basic injustice which all the racial, sexual and ethnic quota systems don't touch at all. In this framework, minority quotas are simply a way for minorities to get their piece of the action in this unjust meritocratic system of determining who is human and who is not. This is understandable and even morally commendable, but it leaves untouched the problem of the lack of respect in America for the individual human being, however poor and talentless he may be.

This pessimistic diagnosis of the state of equalitarianism in America weakens the argument for reverse racial and sexual discrimination. The argument from strict justice is less persuasive, at any rate. However, the arguments from social utility remain valid and strong. And if women and blacks are favored, it is inevitable that whites and males will be discriminated against, as was pointed out above. But as we conclude this treatment of reverse discrimination, let's note one very important difference between this latter compensatory discrimination, and the former "unjust" discrimination. When blacks and women are kept out of the American mainstream, it is a blow to their self-esteem. We inevitably regard ourselves as others regard us. We behave as we are expected to behave. And as long as women and blacks were expected to be and to act as inferior and as less than human, they tended to live out their lives in such an inferior role. The phenomenon of "the self-fulfilling prophecy" is a fact of human behavior. In this, more than in anything else, consists the viciousness of unjust discrimination. It makes persons relegate themselves to the realm of the subhuman. Compensatory discrimination has, for example, no such effect on whites or males. These belong to the favored group. Their self-esteem is relatively secure. Though in a sense they are the new "victims" they are not victims in the sense that blacks and women were and often still are. Reverse discrimination does not touch on their humanity. The goal of reverse discrimination is not a system in which every subgroup will be proportionately represented in every area of human life. The goal is rather that every individual will have the opportunity to be viewed, and to view himself, as the human equal of every other human.

It would take nothing less than a revolution, however, to break the automatic link in America between productivity, money and humanness. Our system of taxation, our salary structure, and most importantly, our materialistic goals would have to be profoundly altered. Reformed college admissions policies and preferential hiring don't touch the surface of *this* problem.

CONCLUSION

This chapter has confined itself to the relatively manageable problem of the justice-scene within U.S. borders. First, we saw that discrimination is not necessarily a moral no-no. It is perfectly just, and in fact obligatory, to respect the merit, talent and uniqueness of individuals. This is another way of saying that discrimination is a moral obligation. It becomes immoral when it ceases to respect basic human equality. (This chapter is based on a philosophy of man that recognizes no master race or superior sexual caste.) Equalitarian justice comes first, even in a meritocracy.

Second, we saw that when rigid application of norms of merit effectively introduces a caste system which accords subhuman treatment to some groups of persons, then reverse discrimination may be called for, at least until human equality is restored. Merit isn't everything. This remedy has been urged in favor of black, Puerto Rican, Indian, and female "minorities."

Third, we saw that in U.S. society, meritocratic bias may be a more fundamental problem of justice than racial or sexual bias. Economic reward and consequent human treatment must be earned in America. The beautiful, the talented, and the rich are honored regardless of race or sex. The poor, the ugly, and the untalented are stepped on regardless of race or sex. Reverse discrimination may serve to get minorities into the meritocratic spoils system itself. So maybe reverse discrimination is best defended in terms of social utility rather than of strict justice.

Of course, we have barely scratched the surface of the injustices seething in today's world. How long, for example, will the inhabitants of the "Third World" allow themselves to be exploited and degraded as human beings? How would you apply to this case the above considerations of merit and equality, of discrimination and reverse discrimination? These principles look harmless enough, perhaps, against the backdrop of the domestic scene. But their application to the international scene would require nothing short of a profound and shattering revolution, a revolution that many believe is now in the making. After reading this chapter, return to the "Justice IQ" in the beginning. How do those statements look to you now?

Justice guarantees the impersonal basic minimum that I need to develop as a human being. "Give us justice," say the oppressed minorities; "we don't want your love; we don't care if you hate us." And indeed I owe justice to those I dislike, and to those whom I don't even know. Justice is the basic indispensable minimum of human relations. We come next to the equally important personal dimension of human relations. I need justice simply to *exist* as a human being, but I need love to *grow* as a human being. We turn now to a consideration of human love and, in particular, of human sexual love.

TEN: THE SEXES

Nothing is so much to be shunned as sex relations.

St. Augustine

And what's the point of revolution
Without general copulation?

Weiss[1]

All the lonely people—
Where do they all come from?

Lennon and McCartney[2]

Each one of us is a sexed human being, a fact which is reflected in the way we dress, walk, shake hands, and drive an automobile. All human activity and creativity have been traced back to the sexual libido. At the risk of distorting this pansexual dimension of human living, this chapter adopts a much narrower focus on sexual behavior. We will discuss not sexuality in general, but rather some of the moral issues raised by the use of genital sex. And this makes sense. Society does not show much moral concern about how a man's way of laughing, for example, differs from a woman's. But for its own good or bad reasons, society does seem to be morally preoccupied, if not obsessed,

161

with the question of who is sleeping with whom. Our very language reflects this obsession. When we say that a woman has good morals or bad morals we are not referring to her attitudes toward justice, ecology, or the morality of war. "Morality," in common parlance, is identified with the conventional code of sexual behavior, and more specifically, genital behavior.

Even this narrow net of genitality catches a lot of moral fish. Under this heading are comprised issues like the meaning of marriage, homosexuality, trial marriage, engagement, procreation, birth control, artificial insemination, prostitution, and the list could go on. We will not discuss each of these issues in its own right. Rather, we will outline three popular and current "philosophies of human sexuality." In the light of these three fameworks you can draw your own moral conclusions about what types of behavior are most faithful to what it means to be a sexual human being. So the chapter discusses in turn what we will call (1) holistic sex, (2) relational sex, and (3) recreational sex. But first, to get your own thoughts going, take a preliminary test of your present attitudes about sexual ethics.

Your Philosophy of Human Sexuality

Which of the following three positions comes closest to your philosophy of human sexuality?

Holistic Sex: Sex is a complex reality involving at least four dimensions which need to be taken responsibly into account. These are (1) the *biological* (the mutual male-female complementarity, structure and needs), (2) the *interpersonal* (mutual loving commitment and mutual fostering of personal growth), (3) the *procreational* (responsible decision about whether or not to have children who are the expression of parental love), and (4) the *social* or *public* (the commitment, as not clandestine but public, involves legal, familial, and sometimes religious responsibilities). When any dimension is ignored, the whole reality becomes distorted.

Relational Sex: Sex is total intimacy between two persons. Without fear of being unfaithful to the realities of human sexuality, they may express their sexuality in any way they choose within the context of their commitment. They might invite a third party to share their marital relations. Or a homosexual couple, for example, might adopt children. There are no dimensions of human sexual reality that demand responsible consideration as holistic sex philosophy claims, except the mutually honest and loving commitment of the persons involved.

Recreational or "Uncommitted" Sex: The reality of human sexuality is in no way distorted by its casual use for pleasure, physiological release, or sport. The experience can be impersonal or personal, but the focus is on pleasure and satisfaction without personal commitment. No other dimensions of human sexuality need be taken into account to avoid distortion of the realities involved.

Would you expect or hope that your date share your general view? Your fiance? Your spouse? Your son? Your daughter?

Do you believe in the "double standard" of sexual morality?

Could you in perfect good conscience follow now one, and now another of the three above philosophies? Would the fact of whether or not you were married change your answer?

What philosophy of human sexuality is implied by each of the following statements? Check the ones with which you agree.

1. Homosexuality is a disease to be sympathetically tolerated, but not a valid human ideal to be openly fostered and encouraged.

2. Marriage is a purely private commitment between two people. I intend to get married without benefit of clergy or license or ceremony.

3. Marriage is a one-to-one commitment which would be violated by extramarital affairs.

4. Either partner should be free to terminate the marriage without legal penalty whenever he or she chooses.

5. No children without marriage.

6. Being engaged is no different from being officially married.

7. Every marriage, before becoming permanent, should be preceded by a two-year trial marriage period.

8. Alimony is an anachronism in the world of women's liberation.

9. Every couple, without interference from the state or the church, has the right to have as few or as many children as they please.

10. Sexual intercourse without commitment is immoral.

11. In sex, anything goes as long as there is mutual consent and no harm done.

12. Statement 11 applies to fifteen-year-olds on up.

13. Marriage vows should be "until death do us part." (If

you disagree with this, re-word the vow: "until _____ do us part.")

HOLISTIC SEX

Did you find yourself agreeing with those statements which reflect a holistic view of sex (chiefly statements 1, 3, 5, 11, 13, and maybe 8 and 9)? If so, you stand on the more traditional and conservative side of sexual morality. A holistic view is one that tries to take in the whole picture. Sex has many aspects. And holism claims that no one aspect may be ignored with impunity. There is a *biological* side to sex as well as an *interpersonal* side. Sex is involved with *procreation*, and it has a *public* and legal dimension to it as well. In other words, sex is not simple. It is a complex reality. To close one's eyes to any aspect of it is to be unfaithful to that reality, and hence immoral. The four dimensions are interrelated. To neglect one is to distort the whole. Let's consider in turn each of these four connected dimensions of human sexuality.

The Four Dimensions of Sexuality

The Biological Dimension: The use of sexuality cannot morally be left to the purely subjective whim or decision of the parties involved. This is the primary thrust of holistic sex philosophy. There are some objectives given which demand to be responsibly taken into account. The most basic among these is the not very startling fact that the human race is divided into males and females in roughly equal numbers. Though this biological fact is obvious, it is not without ethical significance—regarding the issue of homosexuality, for example.

Biologically, there are two sexes. Their attraction and complementarity are common to all cultures. Their sexual cooperation is essential to the survival of the species. Heterosexuality then is more than a cultural accident or a conventionally defined ideal. This is not an argument for social prejudice or legal sanctions against homosexuals. Nor does it claim that the homosexual is inherently immoral. The bipolar character of human sexuality simply challenges the adequacy of extolling homosexuality as a valid human ideal on a par with heterosexuality.

In this view, the homosexual deserves help rather than praise or condemnation. The problem (and it is a problem) is one of immaturity rather than immorality. In the words of Freud: "It is a variation of the sexual function produced by a certain arrest of sexual development." Whereas most children, after a stage of homosexual attraction, pass on to interest in the opposite sex, the homosexual for emotional and environmental reasons remains fixated at the earlier stage. When the homosexual overtly lives out this less than ideal sexual life-style, his actions are to be no more morally condemned than actions which flow from other types of immature neurotic patterns. Biological holism is not a vote against the homosexual but rather a vote for the ideal of heterosexuality as the fundamental shape that human sexual relations should take since this is most consonant with the reality involved.

The Interpersonal Dimension: It is this dimension that sets human sexuality apart from that of the subhuman animal. Human sex (we're speaking morally now) is not mindless procreation. Nor is it the impersonal pursuit of pleasure. Of course, it *can* be exercised in these animal ways, but only at the cost of ignoring the personalism which makes human sexuality unique. "Commitment" is the key. The biological and procreative sides of sex are at the service of *persons* who are committed to each other in mutual love and mutual growth. Sex without such commitment is a pale and distorted imitation of the richness, beauty and potentiality of the real thing. It is loving commitment that brings this potential to full flower.

This is not to say that all is sweetness and light. "Love," says James Thurber, "is what we've been through together," through the mill, most likely, over and over again, and in various ever unexpected ways. Romantic feeling is the least of it. Commitment is an act of will. I choose the other as a *value* (see Chapter One). He or she becomes part of my whole life pattern, part of myself. The archetypal paragon of such commitment would be the man and wife who have managed to spend a life growing together and raising a family together. We'll leave open, however, the question of sexual intercourse without marriage. Here's why.

Commitment is an evolving kind of thing. Even to make a date is a kind of promise, a sort of minor commitment to another. To be a friend is a more demanding commitment. Commitment grows as a couple thinks about becoming engaged. It becomes deeper still when they make their intentions public and announce their plans for marriage. The public ratification of this commitment on the wedding day, the subsequent crises of money, child-raising, family disasters big and small, as well as satisfactions shared, pleasures enjoyed, and finally the simple fact of being at home together with each other—all these signal the ever-deepening evolution of what we have called their mutual loving commitment.

Holistic sex need not set down any hard and fast rules about the degree of sexual intimacy appropriate to each stage of the evolving commitment. It says only that there is a link between the two. Sexual intercourse without commitment is a distortion of this reality. In particular, holistic sex need not get locked into the "magic-moment" box. The magic moment theory would say that until one minute before the wedding ceremony, the couple must act as "brother and sister," but that one moment after, "anything goes." What is called fornication at 4:59 P.M. before the ceremony is smiled on by the whole world at 5:01 P.M. This view seems ludicrous precisely because it does not do justice to the gradual way that persons grow together. On the other hand, it is perfectly consistent, even with this evolving view of holistic sex, for a couple to wait for the public ratification of their commitment (the ceremony) before celebrating it by complete physical intimacy. Wedding night virgins and their male counterparts may well be in the minority, but in the holistic view they are certainly not ridiculous.

The Procreative Dimension: The complex reality of human sexuality demands recognition as bipolar and as interpersonal. Homosexuality does not do justice to the first of these dimensions. And uncommitted sex distorts the second. There is a third dimension to human sexuality, equally demanding respect and equally unstartling, viz., the procreative. In other words, heterosexual intercourse has something to do with babies. It would seem silly to even mention this except for the widespread irresponsibility in this area of sexual relations. Holistic sex demands that a couple make a responsible decision about children.

There's more than one way of being irresponsible here. One thinks of adolescents thoughtlessly experimenting, unconcerned about the possible procreative consequences of their behavior. Or how about a husband who would risk conceiving a child when a pregnancy could seriously injure the health of his wife? And does such behavior become less irresponsible when it is done in the spirit of "trusting God" to take care of the consequences? Or, for a final example, how responsible would it be to organize an anti-birth control campaign in countries where over-population is causing the deaths of hundreds of thousands of people? These examples are all refusals to consider responsible limits on procreation.

Of course, refusal to procreate can be irresponsible too. What would you think of the wife who won't even discuss with her husband the question of having a child? Responsible parenthood cuts both ways. Holistic sex is not out to either maximize or minimize the baby population. Nor does it necessarily advocate artificial contraception. The holistic view is simply this. Among fertile couples, at least, procreativity is an essential dimension of sexuality. You distort the whole relationship when you ignore this and refuse to take it responsibly into account. Procreation cannot with impunity be separated from heterosexuality and commitment. The biological and personal disasters from millions of abortions bear witness to this, as do many childless, loveless marriages which end in divorce.

Of course, couples will differ in the ways that they choose to exercise procreative responsibility. For many, the answer will be artificial contraception in order to limit the number of children, space them, or preclude offspring altogether. Others might practice periodic abstinence from sexual intercourse for the same ends. Others, still, may have recourse to sterilization after they have had the number of children for whom they can responsibly care. Finally, there are couples who will decide for religious reasons that it is irresponsible to interfere in any way with the natural course of procreation. Holistic sex philosophy simply makes the minimal claim that procreativity is bound up with sexuality, and that to ignore this is to endanger the health and integrity of the whole relationship.

The Socio-Public Dimension. This complex, heterosexual, interpersonal, procreative reality is not a purely private affair between the two partners involved. The relationship, while highly personal, has a public social aspect to it. There are responsibilities to the wider community. A clandestine relationship becomes morally distorted, says holistic philosophy. It is no accident that other people are very interested in who is sleeping with whom. Further than that, society goes to great lengths to control and determine who *may* sleep with whom.

This socio-legal side to sexuality is probably the one aspect that varies the most from culture to culture. But in one form or another it is present in all of them. Even in the typically fragmented American family situation, you don't merely marry a partner, but you marry into a whole new family. In other civilizations you marry a tribe, and among royalty of yesteryear you could marry a whole kingdom. For most people, there is no escape from in-laws.

And the state brings its own pressures to bear upon this very personal relationship. It issues licenses, administers tests for venereal disease, sets up criteria for separation and divorce, and decides on inheritances. There are proposals even now being made for the state to determine who may and who may not have children, and how many. However offensive this all seems to those involved in the private intimacies of romantic love, their private sexual doings are very much a matter of public concern. And any relationship that does not responsibly take this very real social dimension into account is bound to become morally distorted says holistic sex philosophy.

The cultural, legal, and religious conventions, laws and taboos surrounding sexual behavior are deeply rooted in human biology. What is here at stake is our survival as a species. Sex is not fun and games. Sex is wrapped up with the future existence of the race. The human life system is not indestructible. There are ecological imperatives to be obeyed. Holism roots itself solidly in respect for these complexities. In complexity lies health, and in ethics health is the synonym for morality.

RELATIONAL SEX

As we have just seen, holism views sexuality as a complex objective reality. Like it or not, there are objective given factors to be reckoned with, and these will not go away just because you want them to. Sexual morality, then, consists in facing and respecting these factors. So much for holism. Relational sexual philosophy is a whole new moral ball game. The focus is shifted away from objectivity and toward subjectivity. The rule is this: Sex is whatever the couple chooses to make it. There is only one given, namely, the mutually honest and loving commitment of the persons or couple involved. Granting this, then without fear of being unfaithful to the realities of human sexuality, they may express their sexuality in any way they choose within the context of their commitment.

Interpersonal Commitment Is the Key

Relational sex is a kind of Sartrean subjectivity (Sartreanism à deux!). It's not new rules for the old sex ball game. It's an entirely new ball game. New, however, does not mean irresponsible. The realities of sex receive an entirely different interpretation in the relational view. What was true of human sexuality in the past is simply not the case any longer, or need not be the case. Relational sex does not want to distort the dimensions that holism holds sacred. Relational sex says, rather, that some of these dimensions are not pertinent anymore. Scientific advances in the area of procreation have changed the realities and hence removed some of the consequent responsibilities. The result is that we have many more alternative moral ways of shaping our sexual lives than we have ever had before. We might say that there's been a change in "the facts of life." Two facts especially stand out: (1) we can now have sex without babies; and (2) soon we can think of having babies without sex! Let's consider each of these in turn.

The relational philosophy that we are now considering claims that holistic sex is locked into the hyphenated sex-plus-procreation box. The single greatest reason for the modern sexual revolution has been the break in this link between sex and procreation. First—and this is no news—we can have sex without babies. The variety and availability of birth control techniques leave no doubt on that score. And these are being constantly improved upon for both males and females.

And, more dramatically, the converse is also true. We can have babies without sex. Artificial insemination of sperm from the husband, from another man, or from a sperm bank has long been with us. Techniques are now being developed to fertilize a woman's ovum in a test tube and transplant the resultant embryo to her womb or to another woman's womb. The process called "cloning" bypasses egg, sperm, sexual intercourse, and fertilization altogether, triggering by asexual means the development of an embryo from a single cell. In Chapter Eight we considered such genetic experiments from the viewpoint of respect for human life, especially human foetal life. Now we look at the consequences implied for the morality of human sexual behavior.

Sex without babies; babies without sex: what's the conclusion? Simply this. Sexual activity and reproduction need no longer be lumped together under one set of moral norms, as holism pretends. Relational sex philosophy claims that most of the holistic taboos are throwbacks to a time when sex had an inevitable link with procreation, and when, accordingly, moral norms were set with a view to children. Children need a stable family. Therefore it was felt that sexual activity should be confined to a stable marital relationship. The laws governing marriage, the taboos against homosexuality, all had in view this concern with procreation. But now that the link between sex and procreation has been broken, there is no need to link together holism's four dimensions: the biological, the interpersonal, the procreational, and the socio-public. It is morally responsible now to consider sexual activity and reproduction as *separate* and *independent* moral issues. Holism can no longer get away with building a procreative fence around sexual moral norms. In fact, if sexual activity is considered on its own merits alone, only one of holism's four dimensions remains relevant, namely, interpersonal commitment. And it is in the context of this dimension alone that relational sex philosophy takes its stand.

Sexual norms are anchored now solely on the responsible, loving, honest decisions mutually arrived at by the persons concerned. Heterosexuality, procreative taboos, and social conventions are no longer to be automatically normative. It is up to the couple (homosexual or heterosexual) to determine responsibly how they will shape and determine the sexual side of their lives. The break between sex and reproduction has opened up alternatives for responsible sexual expression which in the past would have been either impossible or irresponsible.

We are now free, say the relationists, to consider trial marriages, group marriages, and polygamy for the elderly. (If women outlive men, the argument goes, why shouldn't two older ladies live out their declining years in physical comfort and intimacy with an older man?) Homosexual marriages, bigamy, polyandry, and serial polygamy (i.e., the American way of divorce and remarriage) are all viable alternatives if procreation is excluded from the picture. So is celibacy, for that matter![3]

And as it becomes more possible to have babies without sexual intercourse, then there comes up for consideration a wealth of alternative ways to reproduce and rear children. Relational sex philosophy would be open to evaluting the possibility of single parents, professional breeders of children, and professional rearers of children. As a matter of fact, human sexuality is a plastic and malleable reality. Most everything that is possible in this area is already being done. The point of relational sex is not that "anything goes." The point rather is that "*what* goes" is a matter for the partners' responsible decision. There are no other clues or dimensions coming from the outside that need restrict or narrow the range of possible decisions.

Is America ready for relational sex? Officially no, though clearly permissiveness is on the upswing. But, ready or not, relational sex is here. The tip of the iceberg is visible, and the other 90% is underground (underwater?), winked at rather than invisible—which is unfortunate for those who would try to meet the responsibilities which relational sex imposes. It is holism which gets the objective support of the socio-legal public order. So much the better for holism, of course. Since it is embodied in our social taboos, laws, and

religious thinking, it is a source of strength and liberation for those
who can lean upon it. The relational sex philosophy, however, points
to the toll of guilt, rebelliousness and masochism exacted from those
who find holism impractical or impossible. And responsible decision-
making hardly flourishes in a climate of guilt, rebellion and masochism.

The cruelty of official holism, be its sanctions legal, social or
religious, is that it effectively excludes "deviants" from the pale of
"respectable" society. The excommunicates, the relational argument
continues, are driven underground by means of gossip or law or social
rejection. Their chance of finding their own responsible sexual paths
are undercut rather than supported by society. Just who is this army
of deviants? It would include, for example, many if not most
teenagers, adult "singles," homosexuals, divorcees, mothers with children in "fatherless homes," and older people—widows and widowers
alike. All of these people by force of circumstance or choice exist outside the pale of officially approved monogamous marriage. They do
not by that fact become unsexed and relieved of biological needs, but
the only alternative to monogamy that holism has to offer is sexual
abstinence. For these people, relational sex philosophy can function
as a moral bill of rights granting them equal privileges with their monogamous fellow citizens.

What would that world look like in which the shape of sexuality
was determined by the responsible decisions of the parties involved?
Monogamous marriage would become but *one* of many possible responsible alternatives. Relational sex is premised on breaking the necessary link between sex and reproduction. Therefore birth control information, devices, and assistance would be in abundant and ready
supply for all who have reached the age of puberty. Sex education
would be no more under taboo than geography lessons. And parents
would use the same care in training their children in sexual responsibility as they do in the responsible use of money. In such a climate
how much easier it would be for young people to survive without sexual scars an adolescence which our society prolongs even into the
twenties.

The society envisaged by relational sex philosophy would have
no place for legal, social, or economic discrimination against homosexuals. There would be a place for homosexual marriages. The
neighborhood welcome wagon would not bypass the homes of single
adults who were living together, and unmarried couples could freely
register in hotels under their own names. Single males would not be
automatically suspect of homosexuality. The term "old maid" would

fade from the vocabulary, and men and women over sixty who evince an interest in sex would be spared the adjectives "dirty" and "dirty old." We could go on, but you get the idea.

To sum up relational sex, the idea is *not* "anything goes," but rather "anything *responsible* goes." The key is the mutually honest and loving commitment of the parties involved. In this view, unrestrained permissiveness is just as irresponsible as rigid dogmatism. Sexual pluralism is here to stay. The consequences for sexual behavior of genetic experimentation, social fluidity and exploding technology are just beginning to be morally evaluated. Relational sex philosophy claims that it is better able than holism to do the job.

RECREATIONAL SEX

Sex Without Commitment

Holism places a four-dimensional fence around the unbridled enjoyment of sexual pleasure. Relational sex warns over and over again about the responsibility and commitment demanded by the sexual side of life. What about plain enjoyment? Whatever happened to fun? What about sex for the sheer pleasure of it? Such are the questions proposed by the third alternative philosophy, which we have named "recreational sex." Is it traumatic, inmoral and irresponsible to engage in sex simply for recreation? We eat, dance, drink, exercise, ski, and play chess for sheer pleasure. There are no solemn books written about the need for responsibility and commitment to our partners in these pleasurable "crimes." There are, to be sure, books written on the joys of skiing, the art of chess, and the delights of gourmet eating. But these books do not set out to prove that it is morally OK to enjoy such pleasures. That's taken for granted. However, even the most liberal books on sex written today take on themselves the burden of showing not only how to enjoy sex but also why it is *really OK* to do so. Recreational sex, or better, sex without commitment, is not taken for granted as an "OK thing." Even its adherents feel constrained to defend their right to propose it. And so sales of books like *The Sensuous Woman* and *The Playboy Philosophy* go on and on, as if we're longing to be convinced that sex for pleasure alone is really OK but can never quite believe it.

Recreational sex would fly directly in the face of the Freudian analysis of civilization. Sigmund Freud, of all people, would not quarrel with our instinctive hesitation to embrace sexual satisfaction without restriction or reserve. We'll summarize here Freud's thesis. I don't personally feel qualified to pass judgment on it. To the extent, however, that you buy the Freudian story of civilization, you'll have serious reservations about recreational sex as a viable moral alternative in today's world.

Civilization, says Freud, is an achievement wrought by the sublimated sexual energy of mankind. When the traditional moralist warns that widespread promiscuity presages the downfall of a civilization, he proclaims the Freudian doctrine better than he knows. Why and how, according to Freudian theory, did unrestrained sexual satisfaction go out of the human picture? What was and is the result for culture and civilization? How does the philosophy of "recreational sex" subvert this result?

First, Freud's thesis: "Culture obtains a great part of the mental energy it needs by subtracting it from sexuality" (*Civilization and Its Discontents*)[4] or as Philip Slater says in his *The Pursuit of Loneliness:* "Civilization is a parasite on eroticism."[5] The reservoir of human energy is harnessed like the water dammed up at the electric power works. Deprived of its natural easy course down the river of sexual satisfaction, the energy is displaced and funneled into the immense sustained effort required for the building up of culture and civilization.

Deprive organisms of satisfaction—make them unhappy—and they start anxiously running around looking for something to do about it. Raise a little too high the temperature of the paramecium's watery environment, and it starts swimming madly around in circles much like the anxious pacing of a chain-smoking father-to-be awaiting the safe delivery of his first-born. Put generally, a bad environment increases locomotion. It is the neurotically anxious salesman who is most likely to succeed. And it's a standing joke among psychoanalysts that their obsessive-compulsive neuroses are what got them through their long years of training. Anxiety-induced locomotion is a search for gratification. In this Freudian scenario, we are donkeys on a treadmill walking on and on in pursuit of the ever-elusive carrot dangling before us.

The rise of civilization is the reason that fun had to go out of the human picture. In their "pre-civilized" world the Siriono Indians spend day after blissful day lying in their hammocks until sheer hunger impels them to get up and hunt for something to eat. The "natives" in the former British colonies used to quit on payday and returned for work only when the money ran out. Well you can't keep an assembly line moving with workers like that. Intermittent effort is not enough. There is simply no profit to be made unless the machines keep running and the furnaces never go out. So you've got to get the workers to work every day like the machines. How do you tie down a human being to the rhythms of a machine? You make him feel deprived.

This insight, says Freud, was mankind's most stunning cultural invention. It became the foundation upon which was built the whole edifice of civilization. Once human beings invented a way of keeping themselves chronically deprived, civilization was off and away. Now you can't deprive humans of food, or they will die. However, fill their bellies and they won't want to work. Food can't be the focus of deprivation, so we humans zeroed in on the need for sex. Here was to be the source of that steady output of energy that a culture requires, namely human sexual desire, a force so powerful, and yet at the same time so plastic and malleable.

Solving the problem of how to make sex scarce was an achievement all by itself. In the state of nature—that hypothetical world of pre-civilized innocence—this is the only form of gratification which is *not* scarce. The supply is infinite. The paradoxical necessity is to create an artificial scarcity out of an infinite supply. This, Americans have succeeded in accomplishing almost too well. The members of this society—still relatively affluent even in the midst of depression—feel most deprived of all. And so that gnawing need for ever elusive gratification draws them to work day after day, expending that constant and steady stream of energy that makes the world of culture go round.

How did we make ourselves into donkeys, pursuing in elegant livery the inaccessible carrot? Who knows how it all started? Doubtless, the process of natural selection kept the process alive—survival of the most restless, most anxious, most deprived. These were the "fittest." However the contrived deprivation might have begun, it is clear how it is now enforced. Sex is restricted with regard to time. Somehow it's wrong to indulge during the working daylight hours. (It used to be a chore reserved for Saturday nights unless, of course, the couple were Roman Catholic and planned to go to communion the next day!) Despite the earnest exhortations of the sex manuals, the place is limited to the bedroom, or indoors, at the very minimum—or if outdoors, certainly in a nook that is hidden and private. Sex with a partner to whom one is not legally bound requires immense ingenuity, planning and secretiveness. If all these limitations on the use of sex seem perfectly normal, obvious, and right, just imagine what it would be like if there were such socially imposed restrictions, say, on the consumption of food! You'd have to hide in the bushes if you were going to eat outdoors, eat alone unless you had a license, make table reservations under an assumed name to go out to dinner with an unlicensed partner, and so forth—you get the idea!

In America, the myth of romantic love is another way we enforce this deprivation. There is only one man or one woman somewhere who can truly satisfy me. Some college coeds have told me that they begin every morning with the thought: "Will I meet *him*, that one man, today?" To continue the Freudian thesis, the upshot is that we have all those lonely beds each night, all the daytime people wandering around ungratified, gnawed continually by that nameless hunger, searching and working to fill it, their displaced sexual energy providing the steady power that keeps turning the wheels of civilization. This is the answer to the plaintive question of Lennon and Mc-Cartney's song: "All the lonely people, where *do* they all come from?" How strange a sight this could be to that proverbial visitor from Mars—all these human beings living out their life-dramas of tragic, interrupted, and unrequited sexual love, starving for a commodity that flourishes around them in infinite supply, like a man in a supermarket dying from hunger because he can't find any artichokes to satisfy him.

Advertising has displaced the object of sexual desire, transferring it from real human beings to symbolic objects, cars and motorcycles, detergents and deodorants, toothpaste and after-shave lotion, mouth fresheners and cigarillos. At least these promise (though they don't deliver) a gratification which is sexual. More powerful, because it is unconscious, is the pursuit of those objects whose displaced link to the erotic is not so overt. So in our state of contrived deprivation, Freud would say, we relentlessly pursue the symbols (power, money, awards, educational degrees, upward social mobility, controlling interest) which, precisely because they are symbols, cannot gratify. You can't copulate with a doctoral degree or make love to a yacht. So once the symbol is achieved, it withers in my hand, and the pursuit begins once more. Our very language betrays this realization when we speak of the man who is "married" to his career, or even to his car. And so, for the sake of "civilization," we've been tricked into throwing away our lives in pursuit of an unattainable love, and then we die.

Do you believe all this? Society's answer to you is: "You better believe it!" The reasons which Freud gives lock us back into that moral prison we spoke of in Chapter Three. Civilization has us so firmly in its grip and the erotic energy needed to maintain this civilization is so immense that we'd better not tamper with it. In this view, recreational sex is immoral because it is subversive to the civilized edifice which now defines mankind. To be human means to be enculturated and civilized. Sexual promiscuity, erotic gratification for the pleasure of it, copulation without commitment, all violate this idea of what it means to be a human being. In a word, promiscuity is so subversive to this philosophy of civilized humanity that it rightly tops the list of sins. The Roman Empire is the archetypal example of civilization itself when it forgets that its foundations must rest on the bedrock of sexual restraint if everything is not to come tumbling down.

Against such a Freudian backdrop, you can see how the argument in favor of recreational sex would go. This philosophy of "civilized" man is fundamentally perverse, the recreationists would say, and so the morality of sexual restraint that follows from it is perverse as well. Civilization is a sickness, "the neurosis of mankind," as Freud himself called it. Since the restraints of holistic and relational sex foster this civilized perversion of precultural, innocent human nature, these restraints must go. Return to sexual innocence! If this means a return to uncivilized innocence, so much the better. Upon donning the fig leaf, Adam and Eve began a life of suffering and travail. Remove the fig leaf, and return to paradise! Holistic sex and relational sex are fig-leaf philosophies that distort this true primevally innocent nature of man. These philosophies are immoral, say the recreationists. Recreational sex is the path to the true morality which is man's true happiness and nature. Only such a liberated human is free to pursue the realities of his own truest gratification. Unshackled from the ever-disappointing symbols, he can find rest in the erotic love which they symbolize. Life is no longer directed to an ever-receding future illusion, but finds fulfillment in the "now." The holistic and relational philosophies are ways of manipulating sexual energy to perverse and ulterior ends. It is the contention of recreational sex philosophy that it is the only philosophy which respects the reality of human sexuality for what it truly is and is meant to be in itself.

CONCLUSION

The three alternative sexual philosophies outlined in this chapter are all very much alive in America today. Holistic sex comes closest to what we know as "traditional morality." Relational sex is the kind of thinking exemplified by the so-called "new morality." The "Playboy philosophy" is one (rather overly self-conscious) version of recreational sex. A philosophy's popularity is no guarantee of its truth.

Morality is not a matter of head-count. To think so is to fall into what philosophers call the "naturalistic fallacy," which is the fallacy of arguing from what everybody *is* doing to what everybody *ought* to be doing. *Is* and *ought* are two different things. The question, rather, is one of values. In the sexual dimension of your life, what values do you hold precious? Let's recap the values stressed by each philosophy in turn, starting with the recreationists.

Recreational sex sees civilized restraints as a perversion of mankind's pristine innocence. Free, unrestrained, casual pleasure is the top value here. Does this do justice to the realities of sexual living as you know them to be? Would the living out of this philosophy trample on other equally important human values? Yes, say the adherents of relational sex. Interpersonal commitment is the key human value. Casual sex would destroy this precious reality. It is essentially immoral, therefore, to advocate sex without commitment. Holistic philosophy would agree with this moral judgment and go even further. Commitment is important and maybe even the key. But in the view of holistic philosophy, other human values are also at stake in human sexual living. However committed they are to one another, a couple cannot morally ignore these other dimensions involved in human sexuality. Biologically, human sex is heterosexual. Homosexuality cannot be extolled as an ideal without trampling upon this human value. (This is not to make a judgment about the subjective morals and sincerity of individual homosexuals.) Procreation is also a value, the holist continues. The future of the human species demands a responsible decision about children. A philosophy is morally defective to the extent that it slights this value. And finally, social values are necessarily involved in human sexuality. However intimate and personal the sexual commitment is, it has an impact on society at large. A truly moral philosophy must responsibly take into account the laws and social conventions which express these social values. Such is the holistic philosophy which views human sexuality as a many-dimensioned, many-valued reality.

As in other moral areas, here too there is a gap between theory and practice in most of our lives. The theoretical "playboy" finds himself plagued with traditional guilt feelings. The committed lover occasionally slips into casual sex. The stern traditionalist takes a moral holiday. And so in the field of sexual morality, the charges of hypocrisy abound. But this isn't fair. Recall the distinction made in Chapter One between ideal values and functional values. Our sex lives are no exception to the fundamental moral challenge of making our ideal values into a functional part of our daily lives.

ELEVEN:BEYOND MORALITY

Sitting quietly, doing nothing,
Spring comes, and the grass grows by itself.

Zen poem[1]

The all-meaning circle:
No in, no out;
No light, no shade.
Here all saints are born.

Rinzai Master Shoichi (1201-1280)

I used to work very hard thinking and planning. Now ideas come
when I least expect them. If I need to know something, I ask. As
soon as I ask an answer comes. This makes my work and life
very easy.

Omori-san, Japanese inventor
of automation machinery[2]

I won't conclude this book by tying it all up in a neat rational package. You could, if you like, do that for yourself by going back and re-reading the introductions and conclusions of each chapter. The first half of the book outlined alternative philosophical options upon which people have built their ethical systems. You were invited to work out your own. The second part of the book confronted some of the concrete, urgent moral issues of today's world. You were invited to face these problems for yourself and decide how you would morally respond to them or solve them.

To approach morality from a philosophical angle is quite a *rational* enterprise. Even the irrational philosophies (see, for example, "Will-Power Morality") were quite rationally articulated. To ask you to reflect on your own moral decision-making is quite an *individualistic* enterprise. And clearly, morality is very much a matter of reason and individual responsibility. However, to leave the story at that would be incomplete and even dangerously misleading. There is a sense in which morality goes far beyond rational philosophy. And there is a sense, too, in which a stress on the individual decision-maker can be a serious distortion of moral reality.

So this final chapter suggests some correctives to an excessive *rationalism* and an excessive *individualism* in morals. Rather than summing up the first ten chapters, we'll try to undo some of the damage! A profoundly new spirit and temper of life is even now in the process of emerging—and this of course cannot be without its repercussions on the moral life. It would be tempting to say that what follows are some major themes for a book entitled *Ethics: 2001*. However, *Ethics: 1981* or even *Ethics: 1971* would be more like it. The future has overtaken us, although its shape and direction are far from clear. A futurist (i.e., a truly contemporary) morality cannot afford to neglect at least these three emerging directions: (1) the new holism; (2) the new naturalism; and (3) the new immanentism. These, then, will be the themes of our closing remarks. I present them tentatively and heuristically. They are open to criticism and deserve a better defense than I can give them here (if, indeed, they are defensible!). Anyway, here are some possible themes of a futuristic morality.

THE NEW HOLISM

Holism is not an idea that is new to you. Recall pragmatism, a holistic philosophy—holistic because every individual, every problem, makes no sense unless it is viewed in its *whole* context. To see an individual as cut off, alone, affecting no one, being affected by no one, is an abstraction—out of this world. There is no such thing. The desert island is a myth. There is no meaningful part outside of the whole. Nature is not a machine in which some parts can work while others are shut down. The plants, the animals, the air, the earth, the water, the societies of humans, the globe's fiery core, the planetary system, and all the cosmic bodies and fields of force which keep it in its course—all of these are not individuals, but *components* of a single ("living," if you like) dynamically interacting organic *universe*. Morality, then, is not anatomy, where the various parts of the universe are dissected, numbered, and analyzed as if any one part could exist in splendid isolation. Morality is more like the physiology of the universe, where an exploding star billions of light years away registers its effect on planet earth, where a sore toe can give me a headache, where an Arab sheik's oil embargo can bring bankruptcy to an Asian nation, and finally, where it becomes the depth of silliness to pretend that moral decisions are "up to the individual," as if what he decides and puts into effect does not have repercussions upon this whole organism of which he is but a component. The foetus' destiny is surely affected by the mother's allegedly "private decision" to abort it; the lives of the brothers and sisters it would have had, and of its father, are all affected as well. Even suicide is not a purely private decision. Look at the social forces, both official and familial, that are set in motion by a suicide. An illegal football wager can support a gambling syndicate which supports a drug trade which leads to prostitution, theft, and perhaps the mugging of the guy who made the wager in the first place! Moral freedom, holistically speaking, is not standing apart from the whole in a posture of individual self-determination. Moral freedom is responsibly playing one's *part* in shaping the whole of which one is the part. Your parents made the world in which you live today. Your daily moral decisions are shaping your children's world. Your children are not the hope of the future. You are the hope of the future. Your actions are making that future a reality now. Young and old, we are all the establishment—establishing the world in which we will live.

This is a complex morality, not so simple as an individual's following his own narrow path. But health, moral and otherwise, can be defined as respect for complexity and interaction. The human body dies when its individual components no longer work together in complex interaction. Air and water are poisoned, and forests, fishes and people die when we fail to take into account this universal ecological complexity. Stability lies in complexity. The emotionally stable man can play many parts. He has many friends, diverse talents, and flexible adaptability. Being in tune with the whole, a weakness in no *one* part can destroy him. Stake everything on one part—your career, for example—then when your job folds or you retire, you're dead. In holistic morality, "good" is not the straight and narrow path. "Good" is rather resonance with the whole. Our recent macroscopic ecological discoveries are paradigms for shaping a microscopic ecological morality.[3] The universal ecological laws are mirrored in each of us since we do not stand apart from that universe. Such is the new holism. In being responsible to the whole, we are being responsible to ourselves. Here are some of the laws of that responsibility.

The Laws of Holistic Responsibility

(a) "An experiment on the part in an experiment on the whole." This axiom sums up holism's basic premise. Like it or not, we are our brothers' keepers. Like it or not, every man's individual decision not only *can* make a difference, but does. It does precisely because it is not an *individual* decision, but supports and is supported by those of other people in an environment shared by all.

(b) "Stability exists in direct proportion to complexity." The rigid decision-maker, who keeps his moral blinders on, sees life in simple terms, ignoring those parts of the world that he would rather not see. The only trouble is that "those parts of the world" are parts of himself. In slighting them, he slights himself. In warring against them, it's his own self he kills. In terms of the inner world, I can't be a saint until I accept my devils; when I allow myself to feel my anger and fear, then only am I able to practice love and courage. In terms of the outer world, completely outmoded is the notion of man *against* nature, man locked in struggle with his environment. In order to survive, man must treat nature with the same friendliness and respect he gives his own stomach and sexual organs. The simple moral vision of man as separate from nature must give way to the more complex view that the world is my body. In such moral complexity rests our hope of stable survival and growth.

This vital awareness of complexity demands that moral decisions be made with knowledge and freedom. Three laws express these crucial conditions: (c) "Self-correction is in direct proportion to the free dissemination of knowledge"; (d) "There will be progress in proportion that decision-making is free from external manipulation"; and (e) "Vital human interests cannot be consigned to automatic regulation."

Knowledge is basic to good decisions. We have just noted above the destructiveness inherent in decisions made with a blindness which is personal and psychological. The exposures of national, political, and industrial corruption have educated us to similar suicidal consequences on the macroscopic level. There's truth that hurts, but there's no such thing as truth that's bad for you. Self-correction, i.e., growth, is rooted in bedrock reality where truth is freely disseminated. The law against external manipulation of decisions follows from this. Truth has its own unique and spontaneous power. Manipulation is the attempt to deny uncomfortable reality, to blindly channel an upstream course against reality's inexorable flow. So however hard dictators and preachers, teachers and parents try to manipulate their subjects, their efforts must fail in the end. Herein lies the essential immorality of all social and moral *codes*. A unique individual part of this complex universe cannot be codified. A code implies manipulation, an attempt to make things into what they allegedly *should* be. However, unmanipulated decision-making is not based upon the "shoulds" of a common code, but upon the *is* of each component's built-in unique code. Organic harmony lies here and here alone. Like an individual body, a society does best when each component is allowed to play its own role. Each part can then do what it does best. Feet were made for walking. In this view it would be grotesque to require all men to walk on their hands, or dogs on their hind legs, or (leaving the metaphor) to proscribe the reading of certain books, or the smoking of certain weeds, or to prescribe for all certain rites of love or certain games of war.

From these considerations follows the law: "Vital human interests cannot be consigned to automatic regulation." Holism, as we have been saying, flourishes in an atmosphere of knowledge and freedom. This requires that I cannot safely consign to an automatic pilot the flight of my moral life. Routine marriages wither and die. Habitual drug users resign from life. An inflexible schedule filters out people and opportunities that do not fit. I thereby reject the life-forces that are swirling around me, those very life-forces which are myself, which are my own life-force.

Holism's final laws insist upon a firm distinction between knowledge and freedom. It is dangerous to muddle the two, because this could shelter us from the responsibilities we must assume in order to survive. Hence, holism's last three laws: (f) "Values are not facts"; (g) "Unconscious infidelity is as dangerous as conscious"; and (h) "Morality is the right and responsibility to decide one's fate."

To pretend that "values are facts," is to assume that they cannot be changed or directed. It is a *fact* that without the sun, human life on earth would immediately die out. But *I* need not rise with the sun. "Early to bed, early to rise, makes a man healthy, wealthy, and wise" is a *value* judgment, not a *fact* judgment. Facts are what I cannot change. I live with them. Values, however, need not be accepted as inevitable. Values are what I choose. Values I have the power to reject. "Values are not facts." However, by pretending that they are facts, I can pretend to relieve myself of responsibility for them. I can shrug my shoulders and say "that's life," and let my life be lived by values that are outside of me (i.e., let myself be manipulated), rather than consciously choosing the values by which I want to live.

But I don't get off the hook so easily. "Unconscious infidelity is as dangerous as conscious." When a person, a code, or an institution robs me of my moral responsibility without my being aware of it, I am poorer as a human being whether I realize it or not. An embezzler can, without detection, gradually relieve a corporation of its assets year after year. But eventually the farce is revealed. What appeared as a financially solid company is unmasked as a bankrupt shell. So values blindly accepted and lived can give the appearance of rectitude, but eventually the farce is revealed. The person who never chose his life values for himself and as his own is unmasked morally as an empty shell. Hence comes the new holism's definition of morality as "the right and responsibility to decide one's fate." As a component of an organic social and environmental whole, stable because I realize the complexity of which I am the component part, able to correct myself and progress because I don't shrink from harsh truths or allow myself to be manipulted, I refuse to live as an automaton, the victim of inflexible habits, routines, or schedules. I know the difference between facts and values and choose the values which make my life precious, aware that I have no real alternative to accepting this moral responsibility. Even the unconscious "cop-out" is a moral position which will exact its inhuman pound of flesh from the body of my moral life. Such, then, is the lofty ideal of the new holism.

Morals and Mysticism

The emergence of interest in mysticism is part and parcel of this holistic approach to morality. This chapter is entitled "Beyond Morality" because of the emerging reaction against excessive individualism in morals. The new holism has stressed that what appear as separate individuals are in fact components of one organic whole. How does such a component "plug into" the whole? The sheer mass of data spewed forth by ever-expanding science translated into an exploding technology is beyond the rational comprehension of any individual mind, even of the minds of specialized expertise. However, what moral holism calls for is not so much a rational structuring of endless facts. Rather, we are summoned to a sense of the transrational harmony and direction of the whole. Then technology will not suck up human beings into the service of its own inhuman logic. Rather, human beings could use the energies of technology in the service of the harmonies that make up the human cosmic whole. Since ordinary rationality is not enough to accomplish this, mysticism is a transrational search for a human-cosmic harmony and direction. This mystical transformation of rational consciousness also places us "beyond morality." In fact, we might say that for *Morality: 2001* mysticism will not be a luxury for the few, but a pragmatic necessity for the many. The reason is this. Holism demands more than a rational problem-solving approach to individual moral decisions taken one by one. More than this, I must be more deeply attuned to the rhythm of the universe itself of which I am a component part. This is the source of life and energy that my ordinary mind cannot comprehend or put into words. Here is not the place to discourse on the definition of mysticism or on its practice.[4] Transcendental meditation groups, Yoga institutes, mind control programs abound. Their multiplication attests to the demand for transformation from one's own angle and perspective. Here we only point out that to live "beyond morality" is to live beyond ordinary rationality. Mysticism in some form is necessary to unlock the secret of transmorality in an age of holistic consciousness in which past methods and philosophies are not enough.

THE NEW NATURALISM

The World Is Man's Body

The new naturalism is closely related to the holistic view of man, but carries it one step further lest there be any mistake about it. Not only must man be viewed as interconnected with everything else and not only does man exist in a symbiotic relationship with nature, but man is in fact a part of nature. When you talk of nature, you are talking of man. When you talk of man, you are talking of nature. Human society and natural environment are one. To say one is to say the other. This complex unified system, however, is a multi-leveled reality. There are parts and parts; and man is the highest part, the most complex part. The more complex the structure of any part the better it is able to relate to the whole. This is the key to the superiority of the *human* side of nature.

Philosopher-anthropologist Teilhard de Chardin defined as "consciousness" this power of one part to reach out and relate to other parts. In this way of looking at it, all the parts of nature are "conscious." This consciousness can be very dim, limited, for example, to the electrostatic and electromagnetic forces which bind together the atomic nuclei and the electrons that go to make up the stable and relatively simple structure we call a "molecule." This frail, flickering beam of molecular consciousness becomes a walking field of light in the biological world, say, of bushes and trees which are able to interact photosynthetically with the sun at a distance of 93,000,000 miles. In comparison to this, however, the far more complex structure of the earthworm produces a consciousness which is a beacon of light. And man, the highest part of nature and the most complex, has a conscious intelligence with the brightness of a sun. Thus the new naturalism, as seen by Teilhard de Chardin, is governed by what he called the law of "complexity-consciousness." Nature is one dynamic whole. Every part reaches out consciously to other parts. And this consciousness, i.e., this reaching out and interacting, becomes more comprehensive as the structures become more complex. And as the most complex and highest part, man is the supreme binding force, the very "soul" of nature.[5]

The new naturalism immediately puts us on guard against the perils of anything like a *laissez-faire* moral attitude toward nature. It is this new naturalism that has turned ecology into an urgent moral concern. If man is not outside of nature, but is rather the very soul of nature, then in neglecting nature, he is neglecting his own body. Suppose, for example, you were to adopt a negligent *laissez-faire* attitude toward your own individual body, careless of nutrition, sleep, and hygiene, ignoring symptoms of disease, wandering across highways blissfully unaware of on-rushing cars, or driving along oblivious of traffic signals. Your "self" (your spirit, your "soul") would not long survive this bodily neglect. The new naturalism sounds a moral warning against mankind's careless neglect of his own global body. For the new naturalism, as for other philosophies of man, a right morality flows from a right view of man. As man *is* (philosophy of man), so should he *act* (ethics). There is no need for a God or a supernatural power to exact a penalty for infidelity, for immorality. Infidelity to the meaning of "human" automatically produces a life that is less than human. Neglect of nature is neglect of man's own self. The very neglect carries with it the penalty.

So the new naturalism is not surprised at the human suffering that has resulted from the pollution of the lakes and rivers, from the poisoning of the air and oceans, from the paving of our land with highways and parking lots, from the squandering of fuel, from defoliation in the name of war, and deforestation in the name of progress. These *natural* destructions are *self* destructions, because nature is man's own body. These penalties are making us all conscious of the realities underlying what we have called the new naturalism. But the story is not over yet. Experiments are still conducted with reckless inconsideration of their possible effects upon the whole.

To speak of the "whole," of course, makes for easy philosophy but hard politics. As Hobbes pointed out, scratch a civilized socialized human being, and just under the skin you discover a raving, selfish individualist. On the international level, we still live in the "state of nature" which is the exact converse of the new naturalism. Nation is pitted against nation. Each tends to act with reckless disregard for the others. Small nations use raw materials to blackmail the large. Large nations hold the small in ransom with weaponry and technology. But perhaps it is by these very coercive tactics that the new naturalism will be translated into a new politics. Mutual need will bring about mutual cooperation. Maybe the day is drawing to a close when science can be exploited for the advantage of the few, e.g., when the bulk of experimentation and capital is sunk into projects like genetic engineering, organ transplants, and automation, while two thirds of the world is starving, and millions of humans never know any home but the sidewalks of dirty city streets. The new naturalism calls for a movement from the parochial to the global in the allocation of energy and resources. An unromantic look at the nature of the human beast might indicate that this developing global view will come about only through war and mutual blackmail. So be it. Where loving words are absent, fighting words can keep a marriage together. Love is a luxury to a man with an empty belly. To be listless is to surrender to death. There is more hope in mutual hatred than there is in mutual indifference.

Futurism: Myth and Reality

Futurism is an inexact science. One does not prophesy with confidence how the new naturalism will come about, or what the resultant global picture will look like. The facts of imminent globalism may turn out to be far different from futurism's current myths. There is the myth, for example, that we are moving toward an era of increased leisure. Does this myth stand up against the fact of hours spent commuting, moonlighting, attending to the imperious demands of the family car(s), appearing at P.T.A. and Cub Scout meetings, and figuring your budget and your taxes? True devotees of Parkinson's Law, we expand our work to fill our available time. Labor-saving devices to free us for more labor and a shortened work week mean that we put in two work weeks every seven days at two jobs. (See again Chapter One on how your use of time is a measure of your values.) Let's even suppose that the predicted, completely automated production system becomes an actuality—that 5% of the population can produce 100% of the required products. People taken off the production lines are thereby freed for the service industries. Suppose that health care (emotional and dental as well as physical), continuing education, and the opportunity for artistic expression were to be demanded as human rights. Suppose that without them one could not feel human in the same way that today an American feels oppressed if he is without a TV set, hot running water, and a car. Suppose that such services were demanded, not just by the young and middle aged, but by our older population too. Then demands for services would increase more quickly than production could release people to supply such services. Futurism's myth of leisure is far from becoming a fact.

We'll cite just one more myth, that of an increasingly omnipotent government and an increasing loss of privacy. A look at societies more overtly totalitarian than our own should dispel many of our fears in this regard. Dissent, deviation, special interest organizations, hierarchies, competition, and group identifications arise with the regularity of the tides and the seasons in both China and Russia. Neither quinquennial cultural revolutions in China nor Russian labor camps and "mental asylums" suffice to wipe them out. But there is a fear that what cannot be accomplished by force in Communist lands may be achieved by technology in countries like our own. And this fear perhaps is well-grounded. There are the data gathering banks of governmental and credit agencies and the motivational research and propaganda techniques of Madison Avenue. On the other side of the picture, Americans are developing fierce resistance to the media's attempts to manipulate them much like viruses have developed strains of resistance against the antibiotics designed to destroy them. Incredulity, not credibility, is the watchword. The admittedly immense power of the government is more likely to degenerate into chaos than to exercise crisp and efficiently powerful control. It is an octopus whose arms, each representing divergent and competing interests, flail away at one another. And they flail inefficiently and so succeed not even in destroying each other, much less in subduing the population they are allegedly governing.

The perils of surveillance and data banks have been all too prominent in our headlines and ominous in their threats of control. Once again, we may here be in the presence of a myth. What such devices portend is more likely chaos than tyrannical control. Information will fall into the hands of the wrong people. Special interests will use it against counterinterest groups and will experience similar weaponry recoiling upon themselves. Individuals will be inconvenienced, perhaps upon a larger scale than they are today, by the need of wasting time to prove to a computer that what another computer said of them was erroneous. Chaos and inconvenience are not the pleasantest prospects in the world. But they are preferable to tyranny. The free man can try to cope with chaos, where the manipulated man might submit in despair.

We could go on citing myths about the world that is emerging from the new naturalism. We could speculate on radically new visions that might soon replace the commonplace ones we have today. Let's very briefly take a look, for example, at the moon, at the oceans, and at the weather. Already the moon is more than a gentle brightness bathing the embraces of lovers during their amorous nights together. It is a piece of geography, where men have walked, dug, driven, and for a fleeting moment even golfed. Already this luminous aid to romance has been envisaged as a military base, and the United Nations has felt constrained to take measures against this line of imagination. But it is not unthinkable that our children's children will gaze up at the moon with proprietary eyes and see a mining camp in which they own a piece of the action.

The oceans are no longer merely open seas, watery barriers which separate continent from continent. They are vast and untapped treasuries of food and mineral resources. "Territorial waters" have ceased to be mere symbolic extensions of the shoreline. The three-mile limit is becoming the three-hundred mile limit. Experiments are underway to explore the possibility of humans breathing under water which has been impregnated with compressed gas. Airports floating upon the ocean's top and oil derricks pumping the ocean bottom will soon become as familiar as the fisherman's net which harvests the ocean's food. Will our children's children, as they stand on the shore, view not an enormous, untamed sea, but rather a pond dotted with islands of industry surrounded by metropolises where the workers live? Is this the direction in which the new naturalism is moving?

And the weather. Will our children smile at our conventional wisdom that "everybody talks about the weather, but nobody does anything about it"? Space stations and weather satellites furnish continuous and instantaneous weather reports. In fact, we have more data than we can handle or are able to use. For many, this presages significant control of the weather within a generation. And we could go on. Science-fiction finds it difficult to stay ahead of science-fact. What quantum leaps in the area of energy resources are we about to witness? When the wood supply ran out, our ancestors learned to burn the fossil fuels (coal, oil and gas) from which a revolution—the Industrial Revolution—eventually emerged. What energies will we harness next, and what quantum changes will these produce in nature and therefore in man who is nature's most complex and conscious dimension, that is to say, in man who is the very soul of nature? We can conclude one thing for sure. A new naturalism is upon us. Its form and direction are still our moral responsibility to shape. In this responsible task, the new naturalism imposes upon us its own moral norms.

Naturalism's Five Commandments

It is perhaps premature to proclaim ten commandments for the new naturalism, so we'll start with just five. First, *to state man's rights is to state nature's rights, and vice versa.* Moral decisions made on an individual basis are incomplete and defective and to that extent immoral. When I am defending the right of nature not to be raped, I am by the very fact guarding against the rape of human nature. Nature and man hold their reality in common and so their rights are common too.

Second, *every decision to be moral must be ecological.* The first commandment states that man and nature are one. We conclude from this that society and environment are one. Governmental and business policies which pretend to foster social progress, both with eyes closed to the environmental effects of such policies, are defective, and to that extent immoral. Society and environment form one system in which a change in any part affects the whole.

Third, *man cannot be FREE outside of the holistic process because man cannot EXIST outside of the process.* Moral freedom has acquired a new meaning. To think of a lonely Sartrean freedom exercised in a world of isolated individuals has become an anachronism (whence the philosophy of Sartre himself moved in a Marxist direction). My freedom lies in sensitive communion with the whole because that's where my identity lies.

Fourth, *man, as part of nature, cannot be its conqueror.* This is not an anti-technological statement. It merely stresses the anachronism of a Promethean view of technology as the drama of man pitted against the elements. Such a struggle is doomed to failure. In the vocabulary of the new naturalism, it would be a struggle of man against himself. Required, rather, is a technology which is respectful of nature's rhythms and harmonies, and therefore a technology which maximizes the opportunities for man's harmonious growth according to these same rhythms.

Finally, *man, since he is the superior part of nature, should not chain himself to a lower part.* We have seen Marcuse point out the devastating anti-human thrust of a technological rationality (see Chapter Three). It is a grotesque reversal of roles for man to become an extension of his machines, i.e., to submit his complex creative potential to the monotonous regularities of technology, or to hone himself into a superb technological tool at the cost of repressing his human spontaneities. It is true, of course, that no individual can declare his independence from nature, technology or society. But in this dialectic of man *vis-à-vis* nature-technology, man has the right to be more the controller than the controlled. And though no individual can pretend to exist apart from society, society in turn should afford him the climate within which he can play his individual part in all his spontaneous and creative uniqueness.

THE NEW IMMANENTISM

The third strand to be woven into a moral philosophy for the year 2001 is the new immanentism. This nature, this universe, this whole is to be viewed as a growing, living organism. Its evolving shape and form are not determined from the outside, but *from within.* This "*within*-ism" is expressed by the fancy word "immanentism." But why "new"? Well, there's a physical scientific assumption about the universe stated in the axiom: "Entropy always increases." In layman's language, the universe is running down. The new immanentism states the converse. The universe is less like a machine that is running down than it is like a living organism which is growing up, developing from within. The world as a whole is moving not toward death, but life. Life is the meaning of life. The secret of life is within, in the growth that takes place from within, not in some ever elusive external goal. Such is the philosophical standpoint of the new immanentism. We'll expand it a little bit.

The factory that produces a rose is within the rose itself. Life, be it the life of a rose or of the universe, exists within systems, and systems create themselves. The whole is shaping itself, and I am a living part of this immanent growing process. All of us form an organism which grows according to our own inner laws with no need of recourse to some unearthly outside planner. This growth is governed by something more like a genetic code than like an architect's blueprint. The process is one of *adjustments* to the unforeseen problems and dissonances which arise. It's a response to *pressures*, as part confronts part, each moving in its unique direction to the beat of its own drummer. *Signals* are sent and received, frequently with easy, open lines of communication, but often with painful communication breakdown. And so the growth goes on unpredictably because it is guided by immanent laws and not by fixed external plans. The new immanentism calls for an ethics that is responsive to these living internal rhythms.

Consider, for example, the goal of scientifically improving the human genetic pool. The morally sensitive futurist would be more likely to work along the lines of exploiting the life-forces within. He would be wary of attempting to construct a man in his own artificially preconceived image and likeness. It is this latter type of extrinsicism that is heresy. The course of evolution involves inner life-forces whose exuberance could only be confined and distorted by an overly manipulative rationality.

The new immanentism is anti-utopian. It looks not for its hope to a better supernatural world in the sky or a well-planned, ideal, artificial community on earth. "Utopia," such as it is, is *now*. And hope, for better or for worse, lies in the life-forces now present within the universe and in each of us. It follows, then, that the new immanentism rejects the dogma of evolution*ism*, the belief that everything will automatically get better all the time. Pragmatists, such as John Dewey, presumed that if we used our minds scientifically, the progress of the human race would result inevitably. Christian philosopher Teilhard de Chardin shared a similar faith that evolution was headed toward ever higher and higher levels of perfection. This indeed is to be hoped. But the new immanentism does not postulate it as a dogma. The immanent life-force takes many surprising turns as it develops. Species are born and species die. It is not automatically clear that the human dimension of the life-force of the universe is fated to endure and grow. This is not a counsel of despair. We put our hope the only place we can, namely, in the unpredictable spontaneous creativity of immanent life.

The Systems Approach to Morals

From yet another point of view, we could characterize this chapter's approach to moral thinking as an example of "systems analysis." Holistic thinking is becoming part of mankind's logic in every area of life. It is certainly not confined to philosophy, religion, and ecological science. Government and business have found it profitable to adopt this new logic of systems analysis, as the realization grows that all life (including that of governments and businesses) exists and develops in systems. A system is a pattern or network of interrelated and inter-acting variables. How can the movement, change, and interdependence of such systems be explained and predicted? A radical shift of perspective is required *away from* mere *ad hoc* agreements, short term tactics, *quid pro quo* bargains, or apocalyptic goals. There is a preference for attacking problems in terms of approaches and frameworks, rather than of ideologies. Nothing less than a radical change of perspective upon the world is involved here, as we have stated throughout the chapter in various ways. Holistic moral thinking is different, because the nature of man underlying such thinking is different. "Different" doesn't necessarily mean "better." A new world demands that we treat it from a new perspective. The strengths and weaknesses of holistic moral thinking might stand out more clearly if we see some examples of what happens in politics when there occurs a shift of perspective toward systems thinking.

In general, the old perspective (let's call it "OP") involved thinking that was individualistic, atomic and value-ladened. The new perspective of systems analysis (let's call it "SA") is holistic, objective and relatively value-free. OP, for example, was concerned about *countries*. It's "we against them." SA is concerned about *political systems*. Nations are interacting variables in a global system. OP aims at world *peace* and universal love. This is an apocalyptic goal which by-passes the necessary means and type of environment within which such a goal could become a feasible reality. SA looks rather to *stability*. Malfunctions in the global system are inevitable. The problem is how to minimize them by manipulating the variables in the sub-systems of economics, technology, trade, information and culture. OP thinks in terms of *war*. Nation is pitted against nation, and war is the univocal tool of last resort for defense and aggrandizement. SA considers, rather, flexible recourse to varying *levels of violence* which might be called upon to remedy dissonances arising among interreacting systems. The enemy with an opposing ideology arouses in OP a feeling of *hatred* because of that ideology. SA is concerned with *conflict*, with opposing behaviors. It looks for the holistic causes of these disfunctional behaviors and doesn't take too seriously the ideologies that supposedly "justify" such conflicts. In other words, the focus is not on the subjective *tension* (OP) aroused by incompatible goals, but on an objective *dysfunction* (SA), the breakdown of desired interactions due to lack of suitable environmental conditions.

Where *progress* for OP is a "mission," a set of goals viewed apart from the means needed to attain them, SA looks to *development*, that survival marked by continuous growth and adaptation. *Diplomacy* and *statesmanship* are OP perspectives. International relations are thought to be guided by the conversations and decisions of charismatic figures. SA places its hopes rather in the more prosaic non-charismatic *decision-makers* who facilitate systematic *interactions* between nations in terms of all the relevant components. The OP world is one of *events*, discrete happenings provoking unique responses. The SA world is one of variables, environmental changes modifying the whole system and modified by it. OP-*information* (additively accumulated banks of facts) becomes SA-*input* (data on variables that are relevant to modifying the whole system).

For these political problems and categories, substitute moral problems and categories. The morals book written for a new age might not be a morals book at all. That is why this final chapter has been entitled "Beyond Morality." The morals game as we know it would no longer exist. There would be little place for philosophies of man and competing ideologies. There would be a switch of concern from individual moral commitment, to a focus rather on practical social functioning. Moral values, where they appeared at all, would be in low profile, and always carefully defined and limited by the practical means available for their realization. The impossible burdens of *individual* moral responsibility would be lifted from my weak shoulders.

Note well that the "systems approach" to social and moral problems that we just outlined *must* be understood in the context of the New Naturalism and the New Holism. It must be both respectful of that Nature whose law it expresses and sensitive to feedback from that universal Whole which embodies it. Otherwise this systemic relatively value-free approach to morality won't work. The "systems approach" operating abstractly and in isolation can go haywire. This is precisely what happened in America's management of the Vietnam war according to David Halberstam's devastating indictment in his widely read book, *The Best and the Brightest*. Here, I suggest, the "systems approach" was operating at the service of ideology and nationalism. There was no mystical attunement to the Nature that transcends nations, and little holistic awareness of the fact that destruction of the "enemy" was actually self-destruction.

CONCLUSION

It is a complex and demanding enterprise indeed to operate successfully at a level that is "beyond morality." It is not easy to realize that I need not change the world or do battle with the world's evil. Indeed, there is no "I" standing in confrontation against the world. The "I," to be sure, is a unique perspective upon this world, but it is co-extensive with the world. The world's evils are my evils, and conversely the world's good is the good that supports my own being. My task is to put myself in tune with the world and, therefore, with myself, rather than to save or convert the world or myself. It is more a Zen-like "letting-go" of the individual ego than a Sartrean-Promethean affirmation of the lonely "I." The successor to the morals game as we know it now might well have as its theme the little Zen saying:

Sitting quietly, doing nothing,
Spring comes, and the grass grows by itself.

NOTES

ONE: WHY SHOULD YOU?

1. Erich Neumann, *Depth Psychology and a New Ethic* (New York: Harper Torchbook edition, 1973), p. 1.

2. Louis Raths, following John Dewey, formulated this seven step valuing process. See Raths et al., *Values and Teaching* (Columbus, Ohio: C.E. Merrill, 1966).

3. For a total of seventy-nine different strategies for clarifying values, see Sidney Simon et al., *Values Clarification* (New York: Hart, 1972).

4. John Dewey, *The Quest for Certainty* (New York: Minton, Balch and Co., 1929).

TWO: YOUR MORAL IQ

1. Unless otherwise noted, the quotations cited at the head of each chapter are taken from the compilation by George Seldes, *The Great Quotations* (New York: Pocket Books edition, 1967).

2. Lawrence Kohlberg, "Stages of Moral Development as a Basis for Moral Education," in *Moral Education: Interdisciplinary Approaches*, C.M. Beck, ed. (Toronto: University of Toronto Press, 1971).

3. Richard Tawney, *The Acquisitive Society* (New York: Harcourt, Brace, 1920; Harvest Books edition), p. 144.

THREE: MORALITY AS PRISON

1. Peter Berger, *Invitation to Sociology: A Humanistic Perspective* (New York: Doubleday, 1963; Anchor Books edition), p. 63.

2. The explanation and theoretical foundations of these considerations are thoroughly explored in Peter Berger and Thomas Luckmann's *The Social Construction of Reality: A Treatise in the Sociology of Knowledge* (New York: Doubleday, 1966).

3. See especially Herbert Marcuse, *One-Dimensional Man* (Boston: Beacon Press, 1964).

197

4. Mary Douglas, *Natural Symbols: Explorations in Cosmology* (London: The Cresset Press, 1970).

FOUR:MORALITY AS THEATRE

1. Quoted by David Miller in *Gods and Games: Toward a Theology of Play* (New York: Harper and Row, 1970; Colophon Books edition), p. 62.
2. William James, *Psychology: Briefer Course* (New York: Collier edition, 1962), p. 192.
3. Jean-Paul Sartre, *Being and Nothingness*, Hazel Barnes, tr. (New York: Philosophical Library, 1956).
4. This theme of section two is explored in many writings by Allen Wheelis and brought together by him in *How People Change* (New York: Harper and Row, 1973).
5. Thomas Szasz, "The Second Sin," *Harper's* (March 1973), p. 70.
6. Claude Steiner, *Games Alcoholics Play: An Analysis of Life Scripts* (New York: Grove Press, 1971), especially pp. 79-80.
7. Here I have relied upon a report of psychological studies made on this theme. See Kenneth Gergen, "Multiple Identity: The Healthy, Happy Human Being Wears Many Masks," *Psychology Today* (May 1972), pp. 31-35, 64-66.
8. Allen Wheelis, "How People Change," *Commentary* (May 1969), p. 58.

FIVE:WILL-POWER MORALITY

1. Joseph Fletcher, *Situation Ethics: The New Morality* (Philadelphia: The Westminster Press, 1966).
2. A.J. Ayer, *Language, Truth and Logic* (New York: Dover, 1946). This is "hard line" emotivism of the logical-positivist school of philosophy.
3. Charles Stevenson, *Ethics and Language* (New Haven: Yale University Press, 1960). Stevenson's less rigidly emotive approach to ethics characterizes the philosophy of ordinary language analysis.

SIX:MIND-POWER MORALITY

1. I have depended on Nathaniel and Barbara Branden's analysis of Ayn Rand's life and works in *Who Is Ayn Rand?* (New York: Paperback Library, 1962).
2. John Dewey's classic on this subject is *Theory of the Moral Life* (New York: edition of Holt, Rinehart and Winston, 1960).
3. The Brandens, *op. cit.*, p. 140.

SEVEN:THE QUALITY OF LIFE

1. Joseph Fletcher, "Ethical Aspects of Genetic Controls," *New England Journal of Medicine* (September 30, 1971), pp. 51-61.
2. George Wald, "Determinacy, Individuality, and Free Will," *New Views of the Nature of Man: The Monday Lectures, 1965*, John R. Platt, ed. (Chicago, 1965), p. 46.
3. These two statements represent the theme of Jonas Salk's *The Survival of the Wisest* (New York: Harper & Row, 1973).

EIGHT:SOCIETY—LIFE TOGETHER

1. See *The Leviathan* published by Hobbes in 1651.
2. R.L. Cunningham, "Authority and Morals," *Proceedings of the National Catholic Philosophical Association*, XLIII (1969), pp. 155-164.

NINE:JUSTICE:WHO NEEDS IT?

1. From a brief of the ABA filed on behalf of the University of Washington in the Marco De Funis case as quoted by Samuel Rabinove, "Law School Minorities: What Price Admission?" *America* (April 28, 1973), p. 388.
2. Thomas Nagel provoked my own thinking in the themes to follow in his "Equal Treatment and Compensatory Discrimination," *Philosophy and Public Affairs* (Summer 1973), pp. 348-363.

TEN:THE SEXES

1. Quoted by Philip Slater, *The Pursuit of Loneliness: American Culture at the Breaking Point* (Boston: Beacon Press, 1970), p. 96.
2. *Ibid.*, p. 1.
3. See Robert Francoeur, *Eve's New Rib: Twenty Faces of Sex, Marriage and Family* (New York: Harcourt, Brace, Jovanovich, 1972).
4. Quoted by Slater, *op. cit.*, p. 81.
5. *Ibid.*, p. 82. I depend heavily on Slater for the following Freudian critique of civilization, especially as applied to American culture.

ELEVEN:BEYOND MORALITY

1. Quoted by Alan Watts, *The Way of Zen* (New York: Mentor Books, 1959), p. 133.
2. Quoted by Paul Reps, *Square Sun, Square Moon* (Rutland, Vermont: Tuttle, 1967), p. 85.
3. Noted environmentalist, Barry Commoner, has stimulated this effort to apply ecological considerations to morality. See *Science and Survival* (New York: Viking edition, 1967). I have suggested how his environmental prescriptions have a moral dimension.
4. For some preliminary ideas on the subject, see Edward Stevens, *Oriental Mysticism* (New York: Paulist Press, 1973).
5. The themes of "The New Naturalism," "The New Holism," and "The New Immanentism" are borrowed from Victor Ferkiss, *Technological Man* (New York: Mentor edition, 1970) and given a moral dimension.